Immovable Awareness
The Intimate Practice of Zen

Other Books by Ben Howard

POETRY

Firewood and Ashes: New and Selected Poems
(Salmon Poetry, 2015)

Leaf, Sunlight, Asphalt
(Salmon Poetry, 2009)

Dark Pool
(Salmon Poetry, 2004)

Midcentury
(Salmon Poetry, 1997)

Lenten Anniversaries: Poems 1982–1989
(The Cummington Press, 1990)

Northern Interior: Poems 1975–1982
(The Cummington Press, 1986)

Father of Waters: Poems 1965–1976
(Abattoir Editions: University of Nebraska at Omaha, 1979)

PROSE

The Backward Step: Essays on Zen Practice
(Whitlock Publishing, 2014)

Entering Zen
(Whitlock Publishing, 2011)

The Pressed Melodeon: Essays on Modern Irish Writing
(Story Line Press, 1996)

Immovable Awareness
The Intimate Practice of Zen

Ben Howard

WHITLOCK PUBLISHING
ALFRED, NY

Immovable Awareness by Ben Howard

First Whitlock Publishing edition 2016

Whitlock Publishing
P.O. Box 472
Alfred, NY 14802

Copyright © Ben Howard 2016

ISBN 13: 978-1-943115-16-7

This book was set in Dante on acid-free paper that meets ANSI standards for archival quality.

For Jack, Isla,

Carter, and Allegra

May you be free of fear and suffering

Contents

Preface	xi
The Greene Street Feeder	1
No Coming, No Going	5
The Straightforward Mind	9
Wild Surmise	12
Awful but Cheerful	15
True Realism	19
This Precious Human Birth	22
Open and Shut	25
The Weirs of Age	29
Clear Seeing	32
Lost Words	35
The Labyrinth of Exertion	38
Being Right	42
Ordinary Things	46
No Thank-you	50
A Laughing Matter	54
A Space for Contemplation	58
The Steady Go of the World	61
This	65
Well-met in Belfast	69
Lessons of the Selfie	73
Call It a Notion	76
Making Whole	79
Anything Can Happen Anytime	82
Let's Not Go There	85

Yeah, Whatever	89
Put It in Neutral	93
Not Two, Not One	96
Immovable Awareness	99
O Great Mystery	103
The Book of Janet	107
The Silence around the Words	110
Healing is Possible	114
Ethical Attentiveness	118
Living with Dignity	122
Steady Attention	126
True Intimacy	129
The Music of Constancy	133
Soft Eyes	137
The Study of Silence	141
A Mind that Alights Nowhere	145
Give it All Away	149
The Gift of Non Fear	153
A Permanent Beginning	157
What It Means to be Present	160
The Inevitable Attenuations	164
A Time to Let Go	168
One Particular Action	172
My Unexpected Teacher	176
Every Day is a Good Day	180
Notes	184
About the Author	194

Preface

According to legend, the ill-tempered monk Bodhidharma, founder the Zen tradition, sat in a cave for nine years, facing a wall and speaking to no one. In one version of this improbable tale, Bodhidharma's ardent quest for enlightenment caused his legs to atrophy. And that is to say nothing of his social skills, which were problematic to begin with.

In the winter of 2008, I embarked on a nine-year project of my own. In November 2002 I had taken the *jukai* precepts at Dai Bosatsu Zendo, confirming my commitment to Zen practice. Four years later, in May 2006, I retired from college teaching, opening space for new endeavors. Casting about for ways to deepen my practice and apply it in the social arena, I considered chaplaincy programs, hospice work, prison work, and other forms of social engagement. In due time it occurred to me that as a writer and former professor I might best serve the Dharma by making the wisdom of Zen teachings and the subtleties of Zen practice accessible to the general reader. Thus was born my personal version of *samu*, or "work practice": a biweekly column entitled *One Time, One Meeting*, published in our community newspaper, the *Alfred Sun*. Before too long, this modest effort gave rise to a more ambitious project, which was to collect my future columns in three successive books, published at three-year intervals over a period of nine years.

Entering Zen (2011) gathered my first seventy-five columns. Part memoir, part almanac, and part manual on meditation, this book was addressed to anyone who might wish to take up the practice of meditation, or deepen an existing practice, or explore the richness of the Zen tradition. In her introduction to *Entering Zen*, Shinge Roko Sherry Chayat Roshi, Abbot of Dai Bosatsu Zendo, described the book as "a refreshingly unpretentious, down-home account of the practice of Zen."

The Backward Step (2014) collected my next fifty columns, which had come to occupy a genre somewhere between the newspaper column and the familiar essay. In contrast to their counterparts in *Entering Zen,* these pieces presume, on the reader's part, a basic familiarity with Zen practice and a more than passing interest in Zen teachings. More expansive than their predecessors, these wide-ranging essays bring the age-old practice of Zen to bear upon the realities of our present, hyperconnected century. One of the essays examines the imperiled "virtues of solitude" in the digital era. Another explores the emotional dimension of social media in relation to the Buddhist concept of *mudita*, or sympathetic joy.

The present book resembles the previous two, insofar as it seeks to educate, inform, and occasionally entertain its intended reader. But if there exists a doughty reader (other than my wife) who has followed the progress of my thought through the two previous books, he or she may detect, in *Immovable Awareness*, a gradual shift of focus from Zen practice to themes of a more general nature. In several recent essays the words Zen and Buddhism are nowhere to be found. Such modulations of tone, emphasis, and perspective, together with more than a few inconsistencies, are perhaps inevitable in a project of this duration. Whatever else they might accomplish, the essays reflect the momentary illuminations, provisional understandings, and evolving moral insights encountered on the crooked path of meditation.

Yet one conspicuous continuity may be found. Looking back on these three books, I can't help noticing how often the word awareness crops up in my discussions. That is natural enough, given my subject, but it also underscores a conviction gleaned from more than twenty-five years of daily practice. The Buddha admonished us, for our own good, to remain mindful of the impermanence of all conditioned things. But as I note in my essay "The Music of Constancy," the Buddha also implored his disciples to "incline [their] minds toward the changeless." And in my own practice, I have found no better way of doing this than to rest in open awareness, which isn't vexed when I am vexed or sad when I am sad. Meetings end in partings, as Buddhist teachings so often remind us, but our natural awareness abides, unmoved. Behind the transitory phenomena of our ordinary experience, awareness is "the One that watches" and the "One that knows." And if we find ourselves in need of stability, we have only to avail ourselves of that reliable, healing presence.

I could not close without noting that in undertaking and completing this project, I have also relied, week by week and year by year, upon the insights, knowledge, counsel, and support of teachers, fellow practitioners, and readers local and worldwide. To all I express my enduring gratitude. May true Dharma continue.

—Ben Howard
Alfred, New York
June, 2016

The Greene Street Feeder

One spring morning five years ago, as I was watching chickadees flit around our backyard feeder, it occurred to me that those nimble little birds might appreciate having a trapeze on which to perch. When my son was a child I built him a trapeze, and he enjoyed it. Perhaps the chickadees would as well.

Construction was simple. Rummaging in the garage, I found a remnant of 3/4" flat screen molding. From this I cut two six-inch pieces for the top and bottom bars. These I connected with a central, four-inch dowel. Using wire-cloth staples, I fastened two three-inch lengths of cuckoo-clock chain to the ends of the top bar, joining them at the middle with a handsome brass S-hook. My trapeze thus completed, I hung it from a branch of our pin oak tree. Ready for occupancy, it swung invitingly in the wind.

Sadly, the chickadees showed no interest whatsoever. Not on the first day, the second, or the third. I reported their indifference to my wife, who had not yet heard about my project. When she did, a look of bemusement or perhaps incredulity came over her face. She counseled me to be patient.

And patient I was, but to no avail. After another week went by, and not a single chickadee had set foot on my trapeze, Robin gently observed that perhaps the chickadees didn't need a trapeze. They already had branches to perch on. My memory may be faulty, but I believe the word cuckoo might have escaped her lips. Being constructive, however, she suggested I place a few seeds on the lower bar of the trapeze. If the chickadees weren't interested in gymnastics, they might be interested in food.

Although I suspected that Robin was projecting her own preferences, I took her suggestion and laid a few safflower seeds on the lower bar. Unfortunately, the seeds repeatedly fell off. And for another week the chickadees continued to ignore my trapeze. I felt discouraged and ready to scuttle the entire enterprise.

About that time, however, Robin came home from the Walmart garden shop with a plastic houseplant saucer. I could fasten it, she proposed, to the lower bar. My trapeze could become a feeder.

Once again I took her suggestion, fastening the saucer facedown and placing some seeds on top. And in no time at all, the chickadees began arriving. No other birds partook of our offering, perhaps because the feeder was too flimsy to support them. The chickadees had their feeder to themselves, and they seemed delighted with their privileged status.

Over the ensuing months our joint creation grew increasingly popular. Through the summer, fall, and winter, we watched a profusion of chickadees come and go. But when Spring came round again, I thought it time to make improvements.

First, I turned the saucer right side up, placing the lower bar beneath it. Second, I drilled four drain holes, so the chickadees' breakfast would not get soggy when it rained. And third, I sealed the whole contraption with two coats of polyurethane varnish, giving it a pleasing amber glow.

Thus was born the Greene Street Feeder, as we came to call it. Basking in our success, I made a dozen more, selling them at bargain prices or giving them away to friends and family. So far as I know, all are still in use, regaling chickadees as far away as Iowa, Syracuse, and Baltimore.

Whether their owners know it or not, those feeders are also exemplifying the practice of Zen. They represent a principle embodied in the saying, "With people and things, neither grasp nor throw away." According to Zen teachings, all conditioned things are impermanent and empty of self. Given that reality, it is unwise to get attached to concepts and objects, grasping at some and discarding others. "If you truly want to encounter the Way," wrote the sage Bodhidharma, "don't hold onto anything."

This principle is well illustrated by the story of the samurai who was carving a stick when attacked by intruders. Not having his sword nearby, he vanquished his enemies with the stick. In the same spirit, Shunryu Suzuki Roshi once improvised a Japanese tea ceremony in an airport, using Styrofoam cups.

Those tales may seem remote from Greene Street and its eponymous feeder, but the principle is the same. To bring our feeder into being, I had first to release any attachment to my original idea, whose time, it may safely be said, was never to come. No less important, Robin and I had to make do with what was at hand, be it a scrap of molding or a cheap plastic saucer.

That saucer is cracked now, and the feeder is showing signs of its inevitable disintegration. But as I watch the chickadees dart in and out, I'm reminded less of the impermanence of our creation than of the organic process by which it came into being. By that process, I would submit, most of the things we value enter and leave the world, whatever our notions or expectations.

4 April 2013

No Coming, No Going

If there is one indisputable fact of ordinary experience, it is that all things come and go. The bus arrives, picks up its passengers, and departs. Children grow up and leave home. Friends die. Yet throughout the literature of Zen we find the resonant phrase, "no coming, no going." And over the centuries Zen teachers have often intoned that phrase, as if its meaning were self-evident.

For most people, I suspect, it is not, but it can sometimes be intuited through direct experience. With that aim in mind, I would like to offer a simple, twenty-minute exercise, drawn from the teachings of Zen Master Thich Nhat Hanh.

This exercise consists of four *gathas*, or meditative verses. If you wish to explore the exercise, I would recommend that you record the gathas, leaving silent, four-minute intervals between them. Or, if possible, sit with a group, and appoint one member to recite the gathas. If you have a small bell to ring before each of the gathas, so much the better.

Begin by assuming a stable, upright posture, either on a cushion or in a chair. Take a deep breath and gently release it.

Take another and do the same. Then relax, letting your awareness settle into your lower abdomen. Feel your belly rise and fall, as your breath flows into and out of your body. When your mind is calm, and you are fully present, proceed to the exercise.

Aware of my in-breath, I breathe in.

Seeing my in-breath no longer there, I breathe out.

Silently recite this gatha, and all subsequent gathas, at least ten times. You may find it helpful to abbreviate the language: *aware of in-breath; in-breath no longer there*. Maintain full awareness of breathing, noting the points where your in-breath begins and ends.

Aware of the birth of my in-breath, I breathe in. (Birth of in-breath)

Aware of the death of my in-breath, I breathe out. (Death of in-breath)

As you practice with this gatha, view the beginning of each inhalation as a birth and its end as a death. Note that your breaths vary in depth, length, and texture. Closely observe these changes, but do not interfere with your breathing.

Seeing my in-breath born from conditions, I breathe in. (Birth of in-breath conditional).

Seeing my in-breath die from conditions, I breathe out. (Death of in-breath conditional).

By focusing attention on your ever-changing breath, this gatha heightens your awareness of its conditional nature. Here the primary condition is the state of your respiratory system, specifically your lungs. If they are not yet full and are functioning normally, your in-breath can continue. If not, your in-breath must end. This is, because that is: your in-breath depends upon causes and conditions. It is not a separate entity.

> **Seeing my in-breath comes from nowhere, I breathe in. (Breath from nowhere)**
>
> **Seeing my in-breath goes nowhere, I breathe out. (Breath going nowhere)**

As the previous gatha fostered awareness of your breath's conditioned nature, this one awakens awareness of its *un*conditioned nature—what Zen calls its "emptiness."

To cultivate this recognition, acknowledge that there is no place in space from which your breath comes and to which it returns. When conditions are sufficient, it manifests; when they are not, it remains in hiding. By acknowledging as much, and by exploring that recognition, you can touch the unconditioned realm of your experience.

In classical Mahayana teachings the conditioned and unconditioned aspects of our experience are known, respectively, as the "historical" and "ultimate" dimensions. They are likened to a wave and the water of which it is made. The wave is born, endures, and dies; the water abides. Over time we can come to see every event in our experience—every breath, sensation, thought, and mental formation—as both wave and water, empirically existent but fundamentally empty of a separate self. And we can learn to balance those two views of reality, allowing neither to dominate the other.

That is the work of a lifetime, but it can be enabled by this exercise, which Thich Nhat Hanh regards as "one of the most wonderful practices of meditation in Buddhism." What I have presented here is an abbreviated version of a much longer exercise, which you can find in Thich Nhat Hanh's *The Blooming of a Lotus* (Parallax, 1991). Over the years I have often returned to this exercise, and I have found its cumulative influence transformative.

18 April 2013

The Straightforward Mind

One afternoon many years ago, when my son and I were playing chess at our dining-room table, our conversation turned to a woman I'd recently met. "She seems honest," I cautiously observed.

"I would have said 'straightforward,' Dad," Alexander replied, taking my rook with his knight. Although he was only thirteen at the time, he was even then a stickler for definitions.

As it happened, however, father and son were both close to the mark. The word straightforward is a relative newcomer to the English language. The first usage cited by the *Oxford English Dictionary* dates from 1806. Originally, the meaning of *straightforward* was primarily descriptive. The word meant "directly in front of or onwards; in direct order." But by the end of the nineteenth century, *straightforward* had acquired a moral aura, as in the Rev. Griffith John's characterization of one Mr. Wei as a "plain, honest, straightforward-looking man" (1875). If not quite synonyms, *honest* and *straightforward* had come to occupy the same moral universe.

In English translations of Zen texts, the word straightforward also has a positive moral valence. A famous Zen story recounts a chance meeting between a *bodhisattva* (enlightened monk) and the wise layman Vimalakirti, who is returning to the noisy city of Vaishali after some time away.

"Where are you coming from, Layman?" asks the monk.

"I am coming from the place of practice," Vimalakirti replies.

"The place of practice—where is that?"

"A straightforward mind is the place of practice," Vimalakirti declares. Rendered into Japanese as *jikishin kore dojo*, this remark has since become a proverb, closely associated with Zen, the tea ceremony, and the martial arts.

In Japanese, *jiki* can mean "direct," "correct," "repair," or "looking straight ahead." In his commentary on *jikishin kore dojo*, the scholar and translator William Scott Wilson notes that "one element of the archaic script depicts a decoration, or ornament, or possibly a tattoo above an eyebrow to strengthen a charm or incantation." This marking allows the viewer to adjust whatever is not straight or correct. As an analogue, Wilson quotes a line from the *Book of the Later Han*, wherein the "straightforward mind" is described as being "without hatred." Such a mind perceives things as they are, uncolored by anger or other strong emotions.

To see things as they are is one of the central aims of Zen practice—and one of the most elusive. "As human beings," writes Roshi Bernie Glassman, "each one of us is denying something. There are certain aspects of life we do not want to deal with, usually because we are afraid of them. Sometimes it is society itself that is in denial." How can we possibly see things as they are if we are sore afraid? If we are denying half of what we see? And by what means can we become aware, both of things as they really are and of our habitual denial?

The Zen tradition embraces a host of "skillful means," including the chanting of the Second Great Vow, in which we acknowledge that "delusions are inexhaustible" and undertake to "extinguish them all." But no method is more fundamental than the practice of *zazen*, or seated meditation, in which we endeavor to remove the "ego filter" erected by our likes and dislikes, our preferences and notions. Not for nothing is the practice symbolized by Manjusri, bodhisattva of wisdom, who wields a flaming sword. By practicing zazen we cut through the veils of dualistic thought, opening our minds and hearts to interdependent, undifferentiated reality. As Roshi Glassman puts it, we "bear witness to all of life."

For those who practice in the Soto Zen tradition, the practice of zazen consists primarily of *shikantaza*, or "just sitting." By sitting quietly in full awareness, the practitioner allows the lamp of mindfulness to thaw what the eighteenth-century Soto master Menzan Zuiho Zenji called the "frozen blockage of emotion-thought." By contrast, the Rinzai school of Zen advocates brisk, energetic practice and fierce concentration, whether its object be the flow of the breath or the living heart of a classic koan. But whether one is inclined, for reasons of temperament or training, toward Soto, Rinzai, or some modern amalgam of the two, the objective is much the same. To perceive the indivisible oneness of all life, clearly and continuously, and to act accordingly for the good of others and oneself, are the guiding purposes of Zen practice. And toward those ends, no faculty is more essential than a truly straightforward mind.

2 May 2013

Wild Surmise

For better or worse, the word surmise seems to be growing rare. I can't recall when I last saw it in print, much less heard it in conversation. Like the landline phone and the handwritten letter, this old-fashioned word may soon be leaving our daily lives.

Far less endangered is the mental activity *surmise* describes. In ordinary human affairs, the act of surmising is not only habitual but also necessary for survival. Precisely defined, *surmise* means "to infer or conclude from inconclusive or uncertain evidence." And if you have been up for several hours, it's likely that you've already surmised a hundred times or more.

Looking out the window, let us imagine, you observed dark clouds in a pewter sky, and you surmised that rain was on the way. Feeling an unwonted ache or pain, you surmised its cause. Driving to work, you checked the messages on your cell phone, having surmised that it was safe to do so. And when you took a mid-morning break to chat with fellow workers, quite possibly you did little else than surmise, as you exchanged political opinions or indulged in local gossip.

All this is ordinary human activity. But as the history of the word surmise reveals, the act of surmising can also have a sinister dimension. As recently as the early twentieth century, *surmise* could mean to accuse, charge, allege, or impugn. And often the word connoted a false or ill-founded accusation. Those who engaged in such activity, consciously or otherwise, were known as *surmisers*. They were not to be trusted or believed.

A few weeks ago, in the days immediately following the Boston Marathon bombings, our present-day surmisers, armed with the latest technology, were out in force. CNN led the pack, announcing at 1:15 pm on Wednesday that a "dark-skinned" suspect had been identified and at 1:45 that an arrest had been made. Although neither was the case, Fox News, the Associated Press, and the *Boston Globe* quickly picked up the story, all of them reporting that a suspect was in custody. Soon after, the *New York Post*, relying on information posted on Reddit, published a front-page photo of two "Bag Men," who turned out to be an innocent high-school student and his friend. At once foolish and pernicious, ludicrous and libelous, this frenetic activity gave new meaning to "wild surmise," a phrase coined by the poet John Keats in quite another context.

Don't believe everything you read. Don't take anything at face value. Double-check your sources. Revived and remembered, these common-sense imperatives might help to stem the tide of false surmise. But a countervailing force may also be found in an ancient Buddhist practice.

Known as "bare attention," this practice fosters the skill of being intimately present for our experience. More specifically, it trains the practitioner to dwell in the receptive phase of the cognitive process, prior to conceptual thought. As the Ven. Henepola Gunaratana explains, bare attention "registers experiences, but it does not compare them. It does not label them or categorize them. . . . It is not analysis which is based on reflection and memory. . . . It comes before thought in the perceptual process." By closely observing our minds at work, we can become aware, in present-time, of the points where sensory impressions turn into perceptions, perceptions into thoughts, thoughts into conceptions, and conceptions into moral judgments. In short, we can catch our minds in the act of surmising. And with practice, we can also learn to protract the phase of "bare attention," allowing, in the words of Nyanaponika Thera, "things to speak for themselves, without interruption by final verdicts pronounced too hastily."

Those who might wish to explore "bare attention" can find a detailed explanation of the practice in Thera's *The Heart of Buddhist Meditation*, a classic Theravadan text. Instruction may also be found online. In contrast to the simplicity of Zen meditation, "bare attention" is a complex mental process, and it is not for everyone. But in my own experience, this practice can complement and augment such Zen-based practices as following the breath and cultivating "objectless" awareness. And in the digital era, where information is both more voluminous and far less filtered than ever before, practicing "bare attention" can provide a potent antidote to instant opinions, mindless speculations, and premature conclusions. Practiced with diligence, it can tame the wild surmiser in oneself.

16 May 2013

Awful but Cheerful

There may be no such thing as a free lunch, but one morning not long ago I called my wife to offer that very thing. I could pick her up at her office at noon, I proposed, and we could go to the Jet for a bite to eat. After checking her schedule, Robin readily agreed.

As it happened, however, Robin was called out of her office at 11:45. Not wanting to leave her husband in limbo, she asked Kevin, her work-study student, to inform me that she would be back shortly.

"What does he look like?" Kevin asked.

"He's gray and slightly built."

An hour later, over my egg-salad sandwich, I noted that there were other adjectives Robin might have chosen. "In aspect marvelous, in form divine" came to mind, but it lacked specificity. Perhaps "lean of limb and stern in mien"? Or, in the interests of concision, "compact and professorial"?

"But you *are* gray and slightly built," Robin insisted. At which point I rested my case.

In truth, however, almost any description would have fallen short, not because its object beggared description but because description is at best a limited tool. And from the vantage point of Zen teachings, it is often at cross-purposes with one of the central aims of Zen practice, namely to see things as they are. Only by doing so, Zen teachings advise, can we live harmoniously with ourselves, our environment, and other people. And more often than not, description impedes or subverts our capacity for clear seeing.

"Don't say, 'It is beautiful,'" wrote the poet E. L. Mayo, my first mentor in the art. Like the Zen teachers with whom I would later study, Ed Mayo understood that when we call an object beautiful, we drop that object into a conceptual bin. Whether the object be a painting or a geode, a BMW or a sparkling new stove, the general modifier "beautiful" classifies it as a Beautiful Thing, denying its moment-by-moment, one-of-a-kind uniqueness. In Zen that quality is known as "suchness," and to awaken to suchness is both an objective and a fruit of the practice.

Beyond the classifying aspect of description, however, there is also its selective nature. As Zen master Thich Nhat Hanh puts it, description slashes undifferentiated reality into bits and pieces, presenting a part or two for the whole. For evidence we need only consult the obituaries, where the late Herman is described as a hard-working businessman and the departed Henrietta as a loving mother. Or we can turn to the Personals, where Seth and Jennifer are described in telegraphic phrases: "Athletic, handsome, young at heart"; "Fun-loving, smart, attractive."

Only a very trusting reader would take such descriptions at face value or mistake them for the whole truth. More convincing are those oxymoronic pairings that evoke the complexity of actual experience. "Awful but cheerful," wrote the poet Elizabeth Bishop, a poet known for her precise description. In this instance Bishop was describing noisy, disorderly excavations at Garrison Bight in Key West, Florida. But she later asked that the phrase be inscribed on her headstone, as if it embodied her view of life.

As descriptions go, Bishop's is one of the more memorable. But as Buddhist teachings often remind us, all descriptions are as "fingers pointing toward the moon," because the reality they purport to capture is ultimately indescribable. "Fundamentally," declares an early Zen poem, "there is not a single thing." And from the standpoint of Zen teachings, what we ordinarily call a "thing," implying a static and separate entity, is in reality impermanent and without a separate self. The tree we call an ash is actually a dynamic aggregate of "non-ash" elements, including light, water, carbon dioxide, and, these days, the ash borer. To describe that reality as if it were a solid object is to falsify its true nature.

What, then, is one to do? One obvious solution is to say nothing—or as little as possible. But a happier remedy may be found in the art of poetry, which often employs non-descriptive language to conjure a complex reality. In his essay "On Metaphor," the poet Howard Nemerov recalls Roger Tory Peterson's non-literal description of a purple finch as "a sparrow dipped in raspberry juice," a metaphor that allowed Nemerov to "know" the bird in a way that descriptive modifiers could not. "If you really want to see something," Nemerov suggests, "look at something else. . . . If you want to know what East really is, look North."

Not everyone can see in that way, nor is it always necessary to do so. Literal description has its place. But description also has its limitations, and to describe the world as best one can, while remaining mindful of realities beyond description, is a lifelong challenge, whether the phenomenon in question be an anticipated spouse or an unidentified bird.

30 May 2013

True Realism

In a recent column Paul Krugman spoke of "fantasy posing as hardheaded realism." As might be expected, Krugman's subject was economic, his theme political. But his well-wrought phrase has resonance beyond the spheres of politics and economics.

To begin with, it evokes the stereotype of the hardheaded realist—the seasoned, no-nonsense person who lives in the real world. At the same time, it suggests that realism may be little more than a pose. If, as Krugman implies, realism can be false, the opposite must also be the case. What is true realism, we might inquire, and what are its salient traits? Is it by nature hardheaded—and hardhearted as well?

According to Zen teachings, true realism begins with the recognition that suffering is universal. Known in Buddhism as the First Noble Truth, this is not, as sometimes thought, an assertion that life is a vale of tears. Rather, it is a simple acknowledgement that suffering exists, both in the external world and in our bodies and minds, and that we would do well to acknowledge as much. Escaping into entertainment or otherwise denying suffering will do nothing to alleviate it and will probably make it worse.

To understand the realism of Zen, however, it is important to distinguish between two kinds of suffering. The first is the suffering wrought by sickness, poverty, aging, natural disasters, oppressive political regimes, and other forces largely beyond our control. We do not create such suffering, either by our thoughts or by our actions. When it comes into our lives, often the best we can do is bear with it and offer what help we can.

But there is another kind of suffering, known in Zen as conditioned suffering. And for this there may well be relief, because the suffering is often self-inflicted. With each of us the immediate causes of conditioned suffering will differ, but according to Zen teachings, the root cause lies in a fundamental ignorance of reality. Shaped by our conditioning, we tend to view ourselves as independent entities, separate from both our physical environment and our fellow human beings. Whether we portray ourselves as heroes, victims, or merely average citizens, we place ourselves at the center of our stories. And despite abundant evidence to the contrary, we persist in seeing our present jobs, homes, possessions, and relationships as lasting conditions. The words *always* and *forever* roll easily off our tongues.

Reality is otherwise. Death is certain, Zen teachings remind us, and the time of death uncertain. And far from being separate entities, we are parts of the dynamic web of life, where everything depends upon everything else. So long as we remain in our dream of separateness, we are likely to inflict suffering upon ourselves and others. But through the practice of "stopping and looking"—the practice of Zen meditation—we may come to realize that we are interdependent and continuous, both with the earth, air, fire, and water of the natural world and with the rest of humanity. And though we might view ourselves as "practicing meditation," in actuality the vast cosmos is practicing through us. Like it or not, we are one with all that is.

If we can truly awaken to these realities, and if we can sustain that awakened state, we may also find compassionate wisdom arising, not as an assumed attitude or an urge to do good but as a natural consequence of realization. In the words of the Venerable Thich Nhat Hanh, we may come to see with the eyes of compassion. Our egocentric outlook, which views others as resources in the service of our agendas, may give way to a selfless awareness, in which we will no longer regard other people as objects of our aversions and desires but as men, women, and children in their own right. We may come, in short, to see them as they really are, and we will know what, if anything, we can do to alleviate their suffering.

Such a view is sometimes called enlightenment, but it might also be called true realism. And toward that end, the difficult, age-old practice of Zen aspires.

12 June 2013

This Precious Human Birth

On Friday, June 14, my granddaughter, Allegra Rose Howard, arrived in the world, weighing eight pounds and twelve ounces. As I reflect on that glad event, I am reminded of a phrase from Tibetan Buddhist teachings.

The phrase is *this precious human birth*. Its source is the *Chiggala Sutra*, where the Buddha speaks of the chances of being born a human being. Those chances, he observes, are infinitesimally small. They are analogous to those of a blind tortoise swimming in an ocean as large as the planet, where an ox's yoke is afloat on the waves. Every one hundred years, the tortoise surfaces. The chances of being born human are no better than those of the tortoise surfacing with his head in the yoke. Human birth is extremely rare and therefore most precious.

In the *lojong* system of mind training practiced by Tibetan Buddhists, phrases such as *this precious human birth* are known as "slogans." Contemplated and absorbed during sitting meditation, they are subsequently applied to everyday life. As the

Zen teacher Norman Fischer explains, the best way to work with a lojong slogan is to develop it "as an almost physical object, a feeling in your belly or heart." Once the slogan has embedded itself, you can work with it throughout the day, until it becomes "part of your mind—your own thought, a theme for daily living."

This precious human birth is one of four "preliminaries," or cornerstones, of the lojong system, and in my experience, it is one of the most potent. Whether consciously invoked during the course of a day, or allowed to arise of its own accord, this phrase can provide three illuminating perspectives on whatever we might be doing, thinking, and feeling at the time.

To begin with, this resonant phrase broadens one's general outlook. It encourages the long view. When compared to the immense good fortune of being born human, the frustrations and setbacks of everyday life, however real or urgent, look smaller and less substantial. Likewise our petty complaints and hoarded grudges, our habitual gripes and deep-seated grievances. They too look minute when contrasted with the immense gift of living a human life, speaking a human tongue, and experiencing human love. By regularly reminding ourselves of that contrast, we can engender a reordering of our emotional priorities and a renewed appreciation of our everyday lives.

At the same time, *this precious human birth* can prompt us to reexamine the purpose and direction of our thoughts and actions. "Tell me," demands the poet Mary Oliver in her poem "The Summer Day," "what is it you plan to do / with your one wild and precious life?" In its own way, *this precious human birth* poses the same question. And to be confronted, periodically and sometimes unexpectedly, with that question can cause us to reconsider the motives and the deeper meaning of whatever activity we might be engaged in, be it pulling weeds or driving in heavy traffic or listening impatiently to a garrulous friend. In Abraham Lincoln's famous formulation, the phrase can summon us to inquire where we are and whither we are tending.

Beyond these personal benefits, this ancient slogan can awaken us to the mystery of birth itself. Those of us who have never given birth (and never will) can only imagine the pain of labor, which for the mother may temporarily banish any thought of the mystery of birth. But any one of us can honor that mystery, which transcends the boundaries of ordinary thought. Taking stock of the human condition, poets and dramatists from Aeschylus to the present have discerned in human existence an abiding sadness and a tragic coloration. With Virgil they have perceived the "tears of things." And as the anthropologist Loren Eiseley once remarked in conversation, apropos of my son's impending birth, thoughtful people of every generation have questioned the wisdom and the morality of bringing a child into a troubled world. To all such grave reflections, however, the birth of a child offers a joyous, thundering rejoinder. For as the Tibetan slogan eloquently reminds us, that event is as momentous as it is unlikely and as precious as it is rare.

27 June 2013

Open and Shut

There is nothing new under the sun, a revered text tells us. And while the latest inventions from Silicon Valley may seem to refute that proposition, it may well be true of rhetorical devices, those verbal and mental forms with which we construct our arguments and formulate our opinions. First identified by the ancient Greeks and Romans, those devices are still in use today, both in the public arena and in our private, everyday lives. And they can have a profound effect on the ways we experience the world, whether we realize it or not.

I am thinking in particular of *procatalepsis*, a device much favored by politicians, public officials, columnists, and others in positions of influence. Procatalepsis is a figure of speech in which the writer raises an objection to his or her argument and subsequently refutes it. Often the objection being considered is introduced by "Granted," "To be sure," "It may be argued," or some such phrase. By duly considering that objection, the writer (or speaker) appears reasonable, realistic, and open to others' points of view. The effect, however, is to rebut or exclude the opposition, while strengthening one's own line of argument.

As a case in point I would cite a recent column by *New York Times* columnist Frank Bruni. In this column, entitled "Who Needs Reporters?," Bruni advances the argument that in the digital era political reporters are becoming irrelevant and obsolete. Enabled by the Internet, politicians are finding "route[s] around the news media," allowing them to deliver their messages at their own tempos and on their own terms. As his prime example, Bruni adduces Rep. Michele Bachmann's recent online video, in which she announced her decision not to seek reelection:

> It could easily have been mistaken for a campaign ad, with lighting that flattered her, music to her liking and a script that she read in as many takes as she desired. There was no risk of stammer or flop sweat, no possibility of reporters itching to challenge her self-aggrandizing version of events. Weird, no?

"Well, no," Bruni answers, rejecting this anticipated response. He then goes on to cite other examples of Bachmann's strategy, notably those of Anthony Weiner and Hillary Clinton, both of which illustrate "politicians' ability, in this newly wired world of ours, to go around us and present themselves in packages that we can't simultaneously unwrap."

Shortly thereafter, Bruni anticipates another objection: that "you journalists have brought this on yourselves." And though he gives some credence to that argument, he soon returns to his main point, which is that politicians as otherwise diverse as Bachmann, Weiner, and Clinton are using the Internet to "marginalize naysaying reporters" and "neutralize skeptical reporting." For Bruni this is a disturbing development, because it deprives journalists of their right to question politicians, and it violates the public's right to see its leaders "in environments that aren't necessarily tailored to their advantage."

Bruni's points are well taken, but one might observe that in his column he is doing something akin to what Bachman, *et.al.*, are doing in their videos. By employing procatalepsis—four times in a single column—Bruni is himself negating naysayers, neutralizing skeptics, and controlling the discourse. What appears to be a dialogue between writer and reader is in fact a persuasive monologue. Rejoinders are considered only be rejected. The writer remains in firm control.

And what Bruni is doing in the public arena bears a close resemblance to what many of us habitually do in our private, interior monologues. Briefly entertaining ideas that challenge our assumptions and subvert our fixed ideas, we reject those troublesome intruders. Practicing procatalepsis, not as a rhetorical technique but as a habit of mind, we strengthen our convictions and bolster our established points of view. Having briefly opened our minds, we snap them shut again, excluding the possible other case.

To that natural human tendency, the regular practice of meditation can be a potent counterforce. For as Elizabeth Mattis-Namgyel, author of *The Power of an Open Question*, puts it, meditative space "doesn't do—it allows." It "allows objects to come into being, to function, to expand, to contract, to move around, and to disappear without interference." Those "objects" may well be our familiar notions, prejudices, and cherished self-concepts, but they may also be unwelcome and unfamiliar ideas, which challenge and alter what we have always thought. By allowing all to co-exist, if only for the space of single sitting, we open the possibility of seeing things afresh—and of discovering something truly new under the sun.

15 August 2013

The Weirs of Age

It has often been observed that time seems to go faster as we grow older. Our birthdays arrive with increasing rapidity. Shortly after my fortieth birthday, I began to feel as if I were taking the garbage cans out to the curb every other morning. And with each ensuing decade this subjective sense of accelerating time, which a number of my older friends have also noted, has grown ever more prominent. It is as if we were afloat on a swiftly moving river, and each of those "important" birthdays, the ones that mark the decades of our lives, were another waterfall, whose drop and velocity have yet to be experienced.

Yet, from the vantage point of Zen teachings, neither birthdays nor waterfalls are quite what they appear to be. They are at once real and illusory. In his book *Living by Vow* the Soto Zen priest Shohaku Okumura has this to say about waterfalls:

> A river flows past a place where there is a change of height, and a waterfall is formed. Yet there is no such thing as a waterfall, only a continuous flow of water. A

> *waterfall is not a thing but rather a name for a process of happening. . . . We cannot distinguish where the waterfall starts and ends because it is a continuous process.*

There is no such thing as a waterfall? To anyone who has witnessed the power and beauty of Niagara Falls, or, closer to home, the gorgeous waterfalls of Western New York, Okumura's statement may seem absurd. It defies common sense. Yet Okumura is not for a moment denying the reality of what we conventionally call a waterfall. Rather, he is admonishing us to recognize that "waterfall" is only a concept, which for convenience we apply to an unending process. By so doing, we may fool ourselves into believing that this "waterfall" is a solid, independent object. In reality, however, it is a continuous process, which had no beginning and will have no end.

And as with waterfalls, so with birthdays. They too are both actual and illusory. Recently, Isla August Pires, a little girl of my acquaintance, celebrated her first birthday. Her birthday cake boasted a single candle. Not long afterward, my father-in-law, Saul Caster, turned ninety. We honored his birthday with a gathering of friends and a delicious lemon cake created by a local caterer. Those birthdays were occasions for joyous celebration as well as respectful commemoration. To deny their importance, much less their reality, would be an affront to both the celebrants and our common understanding of the world.

Yet, whatever its social acceptance, the concept of a birthday is a convenient fiction. It is a mental construct, imposed by the human mind on undifferentiated reality. As the Venerable Thich Nhat Hanh has often pointed out, in certain East Asian cultures a newborn child is reckoned to be one year old. His or her age dates from the moment of conception. Seen from that perspective, what we in the West conventionally call a birthday might better be called a "continuation day." What it marks actually occurred nine months earlier.

And beyond the cultural relativity of the concept, there is also the artificiality intrinsic to its nature. In absolute reality, every moment is a birth and a death. By imposing dualistic concepts upon that reality, and by measuring it with our own invented yardsticks, we habitually delude ourselves, while also causing unnecessary suffering. As Thich Nhat Hanh observes, in ultimate reality "there is only continuation and manifestation." When conditions are sufficient, "things" manifest; when conditions are no longer sufficient, those things no longer manifest. Too often, it would seem, we attach undue significance to the manifestations and disappearances in our lives, while ignoring evidence of continuation.

"The weirs of age," as the American poet Edwin Arlington Robinson memorably described them, can easily become objects of dread, especially in later life. And the process of aging, which Robinson vividly portrayed as a "stairway to the sea," can leave us feeling vulnerable and disempowered. But by remembering that our birthdays, real and momentous as they are, are also arbitrary creations of the human mind, we can at once address and lessen that deep-seated fear. By recognizing both the actuality and the insubstantiality—what Zen calls the "emptiness"—of those annual events, we can not only see more clearly into the nature of reality. We can also learn, in the words of the Zen teacher Melissa Myozen Blacker, "to blend in with and ride the flow and current of our lives."

29 August 2013

Clear Seeing

Here in the village of Alfred, New York, many of us subscribe to our community newspaper, the *Alfred Sun*. And some us have discovered that the *Alfred Sun*, accompanied by a few well-placed squirts of Windex, can make short work of washing windows. The *Sun* is compact, maneuverable, and eco-friendly. Two full pages will suffice to wash a standard casement window. You can wash as many as three with a single issue.

A few weeks ago, I was engaged in that very task, but the work was not going well. Although I'd liberally applied the Windex and energetically rubbed it off, thick streaks remained. Repeated efforts produced the same result. Newsprint is effective for cleaning glass, I recalled, because the oil in printer's ink repels the dirty water. Could someone have quietly switched inks? Should I try the *Times Literary Supplement* instead?

Moments later, I took a look at the bottle in my hand. In my haste I had grabbed the Simple Green All-Purpose Cleaner rather than the Windex. Whatever its virtues as a cleaning agent, Simple Green leaves streaks on glass. In my effort to promote clear seeing, I had not seen clearly at all. Perhaps I needed to slow down—and to clean my glasses as well as our windows.

Clear, unimpeded seeing is essential for navigating the world, and it is also a central aim of meditative practice. In a recent article Pema Chodron includes "clear seeing" among five qualities fostered by meditation. (The other four are steadfastness, courage, attention, and an attitude of "no big deal"). As Chodron notes, "clear seeing" is sometimes called "clear awareness," and its primary focus is the inner life:

> *You would think that because we are sitting in meditation, so quiet and still, focusing on the breath, that we wouldn't notice very much. But it is actually quite the opposite. Through this development of steadfastness, this learning to stay in meditation, we begin to form a nonjudgmental, unbiased clarity of just seeing. Thoughts come, emotions come, and we can see them ever so clearly.*

Elaborating her point, Chodron observes that "meditation helps us clearly see ourselves and the habitual patterns that limit our life. You begin to see your opinions clearly. You see your judgments. You see your defense mechanisms. Meditation deepens your understanding of yourself."

In classical Buddhist teachings, clear seeing is likened to a clean, still pond, which reflects things as they are. And the chief impediments to clear seeing—craving, aversion, sloth, restlessness, and doubt—are likened to natural forces that disturb or destroy the clarity of the water. Craving is like a dye, which darkens the water. Aversion is like a fire, which heats it to a boil. Sloth is like thick algae on stagnant water.

Restlessness is like a wind, which agitates the water's surface. And doubt is like mud, which makes clean water turbid. At any moment, any one of these "hindrances," as they are called, may color or distort our perceptions.

Through the regular practice of meditation, we can become acutely aware of the hindrances, even as they are arising, and we can also cultivate our capacity for clear seeing. Merely by sitting still and following our breathing, we can permit the hindrances to dissipate and our minds to become open, spacious, and unperturbed. We can allow realities to emerge, just as they are, and thoughts to clarify themselves, whether the object of contemplation be a lost set of car keys or a sudden rush of anger. The process has been compared to setting a jar of muddy water on a shelf. The mud and other impurities settle to the bottom. The water becomes still and clear.

To be sure, this practice may not work for everyone. Newcomers in particular may encounter more confusion than clarity when they first look inward. As Pema Chodron acknowledges, the quality of steadfastness, which may take years to develop, is a prerequisite for clear seeing, especially if what we are seeing is our own narrowness, guilt, or regret. But as the Buddha himself is reported to have said, most of our perceptions are erroneous, and erroneous perceptions cause suffering. That is reason enough to take up the practice, and reason enough to continue.

12 September 2013

Lost Words

As the world knows, the Irish poet and Nobel laureate Seamus Heaney died last month at the age of seventy-four. On the day of his funeral, former Irish Senator Maurice Hayes, father of the actress Margaret ("Maggie") Hayes, recalled that Heaney brought a handwritten poem to Margaret's christening. "I must put that away," Hayes said to himself, "because by the time she is getting married he will have the Nobel prize." Regrettably, the manuscript eventually went missing, Hayes's best efforts notwithstanding. "I put it away so carefully," he ruefully reflected, "that I couldn't find it."

Something similar happened here in the village of Alfred, New York, though the circumstances were rather different. Seamus Heaney visited Alfred University in January 1984 to give a reading. He stayed in the home of Carol ("CB") Burdick, an adjunct professor of English who frequently hosted visiting writers. At the time, Seamus was suffering from a toothache, and for most of his reading he kept his palm pressed to his cheek. Early the next morning, he assuaged his pain by writing a piece of light verse, a self-ironic poem modeled after William Dunbar's "Lament for the Makers" (1508). As he was leaving, Seamus thanked CB for her hospitality and presented her with the handwritten manuscript.

Heaney's poem was witty as well as light, as I remember, though its model is neither. "Lament for the Makers" is a meditation on mortality and a dirge for Dunbar's forebears in the art, the Scots "makars" of the fifteenth century. Toward the end, Dunbar devotes a stanza to a living poet, his friend and professional rival Walter Kennedy (ca. 1455-c.1508):

> *Good Master Walter Kennedy*
> *At point of death lies verily,*
> *Great ruth it were that it should be,*
>   Timor Mortis conturbat me.

In this archaic usage, the word *ruth* means grief or pity. The line *Timor Mortis conturbat me,* which serves as a refrain throughout the poem, is taken from Roman Catholic liturgy, specifically the *Office of the Dead*. It is commonly translated as "the fear of death confounds me."

I remembered Dunbar's poem, and Seamus Heaney's playful appropriation of it, when I learned that Seamus's last words, texted from his hospital bed to his wife, Marie, were *Noli timere* ("Don't be afraid"). As has been widely noted, those ancient biblical words in an extinct language were transmitted via a contemporary, virtual, and inherently unstable medium. Words in cyberspace can disappear in a second — or last, it would seem, forever. Given Seamus Heaney's stature, *noli timere* may well take its permanent place among the last words of major authors. But over time it may also be lost, the uncertainties of literary reputation and the swift obsolescence of digital formats being what they are.

Such was the fate, in any case, of the handwritten manuscript Seamus gave to Carol Burdick. For decades the poem hung in its frame near her woodstove, a souvenir of a gracious poet's visit. When the ink began to fade, CB made a photocopy of the poem and put it away for safekeeping. After her death in 2008, however, both the original and the copy disappeared. Efforts to find them proved unavailing.

Readers of this column may remember that its title is a translation of the Japanese motto *ichigo ichie*. Closely associated with both the tea ceremony and the practice of Zen, "one time, one meeting" reminds us that every moment of our lives is unprecedented and unrepeatable. Each encounter is unique. By practicing with this motto, we awaken to that reality, and we train ourselves to experience each new "meeting" afresh. At the same time, *ichigo ichie* reminds us that what we are presently experiencing will not recur. However indelible it may seem, it is by nature impermanent.

Taken to heart, this recognition may cause us to become better archivists: to preserve what we can of the present moment. But it may also prompt us, in accordance with Zen teachings, to contemplate and realize the truth of impermanence, not as a lofty concept but as an immediate, concrete fact. "For Ben Howard," wrote the late W.D. Snodgrass on a broadside he gave me thirty years ago. "May his nails, his loves, his poems / last." Unfortunately, De wrote that inscription in impermanent ink, and it has all but vanished.

26 September 2013

The Labyrinth of Exertion

Exert yourself. Whether conscious or unrecognized, that imperative underlies our everyday experience. Our livelihoods and indeed our survival depend upon our exertions. If we are to compete, achieve, and contribute to the common good, we must exert ourselves. Even the pursuit of happiness, as it is called, requires exertion. No rest for the weary, and no mercy for the slacker.

Yet even the highest achievers need their rest. The great pianist Vladimir Horowitz was once asked how he managed to play so many notes so quickly. "I relax between notes," he cheerfully replied. As Horowitz well understood, rest and relaxation are essential, both before and during performance. They make strenuous exertion possible.

Quite often, people in need of rest and relaxation find their way to Zen practice. Viewed from a distance, the practice offers the prospect of unruffled calm. Yet, as newcomers soon find out, it is not always easy to rest or relax, even in a meditative setting. For those accustomed to multi-tasking, hyperconnectivity, and busyness generally, the simple act of stopping and resting can be as challenging as the most demanding activity. Admonished to sit still, the body rebels. A shoulder aches; a knee hurts; a foot wants to fidget. Efforts to correct one's posture or relieve one's unease often result only in new forms of discomfort. Wedded to incessant movement, the body wants to *do*, not merely to *be*.

Likewise, the mind resists immobilization. It craves activity, whether that activity be generating memories and fantasies, forming judgments, discriminating between this and that, or engaging in abstract speculation. "Rest in awareness," Buddhist teachings advise. "Rest in the openness of mind." But if we are anticipating a hectic day, or coming off a troubling one, those traditional imperatives can ring rather hollow. It is as if we were caught in a labyrinth of our own making—a labyrinth, as it were, of unending exertion.

Fortunately, a guiding thread may be found in the teachings of Eihei Dogen (1200-1253), founder of the Soto Zen tradition. In his masterwork, *Shobogenzo*, Dogen Zenji propounds the concept of *ippo-gujin* (or *gujin* for short), which means "the full exertion of a single thing." That may sound like yet another form of striving, but it is actually quite the opposite. Far from adding another burden, the practice offers a path toward total rest.

Gujin has been variously translated as "total realization," "total penetration," "total manifestation"—and, most often, "total exertion." The scholar and translator Francis Dojun Cook, an authority on Dogen, explains the concept in this way:

> [F]rom the angle of the person who experiences the situation, [gujin] means that one identifies with it utterly. Looked at from the standpoint of the situation itself, the situation is totally manifested or exerted without obstruction.

By "obstruction" Cook means those preferences, discriminations, and judgments that reinforce a sense of "me" and keep us from identifying with our present situation. Practicing gujin, we wholeheartedly enter that situation, however attractive or unnerving it may be. We immerse ourselves totally, without, as Cook puts it, "omitting even a fragment of [ourselves] from the act." By this means we allow the situation itself to manifest.

Framed in this fashion, gujin may seem to require effort, and in its own way, it does. Can we really allow the situations in our lives to manifest themselves? To be as they are, unaltered by our habitual manipulations? Perhaps we can, but our lifelong conditioning militates against it. Truly to practice gujin requires us to bring both wholehearted attention and full acceptance to whatever is occurring, within and around us, at any given moment. And it also requires us to understand that the present moment, however pleasing or upsetting, could not be other than it is, given the causes and conditions that have brought it about. To practice such radical acceptance, as it is sometimes called, requires a kind of exertion, mental and physical, as well as an effort to counter the habits of a lifetime.

Paradoxically, however, Dogen's "total exertion" is also a way of freeing ourselves from compulsive exertion, insofar as our previous exertions have been devoted to filtering, interpreting, or otherwise tampering with our experience. By allowing immediate situations to manifest themselves, just as they are, and by acting in concert with that purpose, we can allow both ourselves and our lives to be fully realized. As Shunryu Suzuki Roshi once put it, we can learn "to observe things as they are, and to let everything go as it goes." And along the way, we can afford ourselves some much-needed rest.

10 October 2013

Being Right

"I would rather be right than president," declared William McKendree Springer, Democrat from Illinois, on the floor of the House.

"The gentleman needn't worry," replied Thomas Brackett Reed (1839-1902), Republican from Maine and Speaker of the House. "He will never be either."

That famous exchange took place in the late nineteenth century, but the sentiment expressed by Congressman Springer may well be timeless in human affairs. Whether the venue be public or domestic, the context political or personal, many of us attach inordinate value to being right. We would rather be right than president—or fair, or peaceful, or humane.

In common parlance, "being right" often means having the right opinion. And because people tend to identify with their opinions and those of the groups to which they belong, opinions divide cultures, nations, and humanity generally, while reinforcing the sense of a separate self. "When you come rising strongly in me," writes the poet Jane Hirshfield, in a poem addressed to a personified Opinion, "I feel myself grow separate / and more lonely." The need to be right, and to advance one's opinion at any cost, can exact a heavy toll, not only on the body politic but also on marriages, families, and the solidest of friendships.

In English translations of classical Buddhist teachings, the word "right" also occupies a prominent place, but its context and meaning differ sharply from common Western usage. The Noble Eightfold Path, one of the cornerstones of Buddhist practice, consists of eight components: Right View, Right Intention, Right Speech, Right Action, Right Livelihood, Right Effort, Right Mindfulness, and Right Concentration. In its Buddhist context, however, the word right is best understood to mean "aligned with reality." Right View does not mean doctrinal conformity. Rather, it means a view of life rooted in wisdom and compassion and aligned with things as they actually are. To embody Right View is to be acutely aware of the universality of suffering and deeply in touch with the impermanent, interdependent, and selfless nature of reality. In linear representations of the Noble Eightfold Path, Right View heads the list of components, but it supports and is supported by the other seven.

Right View will not be acquired solely through book learning, though study of the sutras is essential. Nor will it be acquired primarily through conceptual thought. Right View is fostered by the practices of mindfulness, concentration, and the remaining components of the Noble Eightfold Path. The Venerable Thich Nhat Hanh explains the process in this way:

> *Our happiness and the happiness of those around us depend on our degree of Right View. Touching reality deeply—knowing what is going on inside and outside of ourselves—is the way to liberate ourselves from the suffering that is caused by wrong perceptions. Right View is not an ideology, a system, or even a path. It is the insight we have into the reality of life, a living insight that fills us with understanding, peace, and love.*

As this explanation makes clear, Right View is a quality of insight, which can be cultivated over time. Through the practice of being continuously present for the present moment—the practice of mindfulness—we develop one-pointed concentration, which allows us to look deeply into the causes of suffering within and around us. In this way we nurture our innate capacity for compassionate understanding.

Right View, it might be said, is the polar opposite of "being right." To a degree rarely acknowledged by those who hold them, strong opinions often have little to do with reality. By their nature they are one-sided, and they are often colored, if not created, by such extraneous factors as political ideologies, party loyalties, religious affiliations, social prejudice, and the will to power. And as our recent national experience has shown, the conviction that one is in the right, however fortifying that conviction might be, can erect insuperable barriers and wreak havoc in one's own and others' lives.

By contrast, Right View is grounded in an intimate, moment-by-moment awareness of realities within and around us, and its fruit is a humane, intuitive wisdom. In Sean O'Faolain's short story "The Human Thing," an expatriate Irish priest departs from orthodox doctrine by granting Christian burial to an apostate, who had left his family and lived with another woman for five years. "Did I do right?" the priest asks the narrator. "You did the human thing, Father," the narrator replies. Such is the nature of Right View, whether embodied in a Buddhist practitioner or in a conflicted Irish priest.

24 October 2013

Ordinary Things

If your waking hours are anything like mine, many if not most are spent in attending to ordinary things. Although you might wish to be contemplating the meaning of life or encountering something out of the ordinary, groceries need to be bought and e-mails answered. Bills need to be paid. Whatever your spiritual aspirations, ordinary life assumes the foreground.

At first glance, Zen practice might seem a welcome escape from the daily round. At its deeper levels, Zen is indeed concerned with the alleviation of suffering, the cultivation of compassionate wisdom, and the "Great Matter" of life and death. Cloistered in their mountain monasteries or secluded in their urban centers, Zen masters and their disciples may appear to have risen above the quotidian fray and to have transcended the concerns of everyday life.

In practice, however, Zen practitioners are as engaged as anyone else with the common life, if not more so. "My miraculous power and spiritual activity," wrote Layman P'ang, an 8th-century Buddhist practitioner, "drawing water and carrying wood." More recently, in her poem "A Cedary Fragrance," the poet and Zen practitioner Jane Hirshfield recalls her three-year residency at Tassajara Monastery: "Even now, / decades after," she reports, "I wash my face in cold water." What action could be more ordinary, one might ask, or more enmeshed in everyday life? "Zen," an old Zen saying reminds us, "is picking up your coat from the floor and hanging it up."

This emphasis on ordinary things and common actions, so conspicuous in the literature of Zen, may be partly a matter of convention, but it is also grounded in Zen teachings, particularly those pertaining to the ethic of care-taking, the practice of non-discrimination, and the aspiration to enlightenment. In ways not immediately apparent, acts as seemingly trivial as picking up one's coat support those long-term aims.

Years ago, when I was preparing for my first stay at Dai Bosatsu Zendo, a Rinzai Zen monastery in the Catskills, I called ahead to ask what I should bring with me. "Expendable work clothes," a resident monk replied. And upon arriving, I understood the relevance of his advice. Dai Bosatsu Zendo, like most Zen centers and monasteries, exudes a spirit of cleanliness and order. Windows have been washed, mats and cushions vacuumed, stair steps scrubbed by hand. Cups, bowls, incense sticks, and other functional objects have been meticulously placed, with ample space around them. By their quiet presence, those objects reflect the mindfulness of the residents and their abiding attention to ordinary things. By treating their surroundings in this way, Zen practitioners cultivate an attitude of respect and a habit of wholehearted regard.

Beyond that, "work practice," as it is called, serves a deeper purpose in Zen training. Whether as monastics or as lay practitioners like myself, Zen students are encouraged to cultivate the "wisdom of non-discrimination," which is to say, to set aside such conventional dualities as "high" and "low," "worldly" and "unworldly," and "sacred" and "profane." In Zen teachings, if not always in practice, raking sand and managing a complex budget, cleaning toilets and studying sutras are deemed to be equally important activities. Distinctions between manual and intellectual, blue-collar and white-collar labor do not apply. By recognizing the illusory and relative nature of those concepts, we can fully embrace whatever task we might be performing, however menial or distasteful. In Jane Hirshfield's words, we can choose to "make the unwanted wanted," infusing new life into a conventionally devalued chore.

By so doing, we can also strengthen an aspiration toward enlightenment, which for the Zen practitioner resides in everyday life. To give full attention to one's work is a virtue in itself, but in the context of Zen practice, it is also a way of opening our minds to a reality masked by ordinary thought. According to Zen teachings, common objects, deeply regarded, can reveal the impermanence and interdependence of all conditioned things. A cup is indeed a cup, but it is also an event in the selfless, dynamic web of life. By caring for that cup, and by looking deeply into its impermanent nature, we can free ourselves from the habit of grasping, having realized that ultimately there is nothing substantial to grasp. And by stopping to contemplate both the cup and the "non-cup" elements—soil, water, air, the labors of a potter—of which it is made, we can penetrate the illusion of separateness, which divides subject from object and the mind from the material world. Should that realization occur, suddenly or gradually, ordinary things will no longer be merely ordinary, nor our labor merely labor.

7 November 2013

No Thank-you

One day last summer I decided to go for a swim. It was a hot afternoon, and I needed both the exercise and relief from the heat.

Upon arriving at the university's spacious pool, I observed that most of the lanes were still open. I chose lane one. As I prepared to enter the water, I noticed a pair of tiny pink flip-flops at the poolside. Someone's little girl had apparently left them behind.

The water was chilly but refreshing. Pushing off, I swam a leisurely lap, breast stroke up, crawl stroke back. I hadn't been swimming in quite a while, and I'd forgotten how pleasant the experience could be.

Upon surfacing, however, I was greeted by a little girl in a pink bathing suit. She was sitting on the edge of the pool, dangling her legs in the water. She wore a frown and looked perturbed.

"Why are you in my lane?" she demanded to know.

"I wasn't aware that this was your lane," said I. "Are those your little pink shoes?"

"Yes!" she snapped, as though the answer should have been obvious.

"Well, in that case, why don't I take the next lane, and you can have this one?"

Without waiting for an answer, I ducked under the floating rope and stepped into lane two. But as I prepared to push off, I heard a still small voice saying, "You're not supposed to dive under the ropes." This time, however, I chose to ignore my tormentor. I also wondered where her parents were.

It's been five months since that encounter, and in retrospect, I believe I might have handled it more skillfully. At the very least I might have seized what educators call a teachable moment. If the child learned any lesson, it was that with sufficient persuasion, a grown man can be made to do her bidding. That does not bode well for her future. More seriously, what the little girl did *not* learn was the principle of sharing, which I might easily have taught her. And even worse, she learned nothing at all about gratitude. I had given up the lane, which wasn't hers in the first place. She might have deigned to say thank you.

Perhaps the absence of those two words should not have surprised me. Ingratitude, after all, is nothing new. Shakespeare's King Lear inveighs against it, calling it a "marble-hearted fiend." Jonathan Swift proposed it be made a capital offense. In my own lifetime I have experienced ingratitude, personal and institutional, in forms too numerous to mention: gifts not acknowledged, favors unreciprocated, service taken for granted. And truth to tell, I have sometimes embodied ingratitude myself, in situations I would rather not remember.

All that said, it is hard to escape the impression that ingratitude is becoming ever more common in our culture. And conversely, the custom of saying thank you—and meaning it—may well be decreasing in inverse proportion to its hollow, formulaic expression in the world of business and commerce. "Thank you for choosing Delta," the captain says routinely. "Thank you for your patience," a robotic voice intones. Like the word Congratulations, the two words Thank You have been subjected to corporate preemption. Their currency has been debased, their force diminished.

That social trend is disturbing, but it needn't be cause for despair. It is still possible to teach gratitude to children, preferably by example. And though it may not be possible or very wise to demand gratitude from those grown-ups with whom we live and work, it is possible to expect it of ourselves and to cultivate it accordingly.

Buddhist teachings offer a plethora of "skillful means," as they are called, for developing "wholesome" qualities, including gratitude. For example, we can become aware of that feeling as it arises and endeavor to nurture it. More systematically, we can practice the exercise, "Aware that I have food, shelter, and medicine, I breathe in. / Grateful for my food, shelter, and medicine" (or whatever else we value), "I breathe out." At first we may feel nothing, but over time our innate capacity for gratitude will grow. In Buddhism, this practice is known as "watering the seeds" of gratitude, seeds common to us all.

In his book *Bringing the Sacred to Life*, John Daido Loori Roshi offers a further teaching. He invites us to imagine an experiment involving two people. One is asked to spend ten minutes each morning and evening expressing gratitude. The other is directed to spend the same amount of time "practicing complaining." In a year's time, Daido Roshi writes, the first subject will have become "a very grateful person." The second will be more miserable than ever.

"What you practice," he adds, "is what you are."

21 November 2013

A Laughing Matter

Last month my infant granddaughter, Allegra, uttered her first belly laugh. At the time she was sitting upright in her father's lap, firmly supported by his two strong hands. Meanwhile my wife, Robin, was exuberantly entertaining Allegra, smiling broadly, blowing raspberries on her belly, and singing "I'm going to get you" as she tickled her toes. Without warning, up when Allegra's arms, as though she were conducting an orchestra, and from her whole little being came gleeful, protracted laughter.

Luckily I had my camera handy, and I was able to capture the moment. When I later sent the photo to a few friends, one described Allegra as a laughing Buddha. Another expressed the wish that Allegra might keep laughing all her life.

Those comments called to mind the itinerant monk Hotei (pronounced HOH-TAY), who did indeed keep laughing, at least in Buddhist legend. Popularly known as the Laughing Buddha, Hotei was a tenth-century century Chan (Zen) monk, who roamed the Chinese countryside carrying a bulging linen bag over his shoulder. Children loved Hotei, and no wonder: along with his personal belongings, his bag contained candies, fruit, and other goodies, which he freely gave away. Over time, the historical Hotei, whose name in Japanese means "cloth bag," became a Buddhist deity, a god of contentment and a guardian of children. He also became a popular figure in Zen brush-paintings, where he is portrayed as bald, fat, disheveled, and jolly. Justly dubbed the Asian Santa Claus, he wears an open robe, which exposes his chest and his ample belly.

Stories featuring Hotei abound, but the one most often cited in Zen literature concerns a random dialogue between Hotei and an old Zen master whom he meets on the road. "What is the essence of Zen?" asks Hotei's interlocutor. Rather than reply in words, Hotei puts his bag down. "And what is the realization of Zen?" the master further inquires. Again without a word, Hotei picks up his bag and continues his life's journey, begging for pennies and distributing his gifts to the children of the world.

Over the centuries, interpretations of this encounter have varied in tone and emphasis, but most commentators have viewed the story as a parable of Zen practice. Although Hotei might be described—or dismissed—as a happy hobo with a generous heart, he is in fact an enlightened Buddhist monk—a Zen master himself—whose silent responses to the master's questions exemplify two fundamental aspects of Zen practice.

In response to the first question, Hotei puts his bag down. By so doing, he performs a kind of charade, enacting in external form the inner shift that occurs in Zen meditation: a shift from ego-centered thinking to selfless awareness. Eihei Dogen Zenji, founder of the Soto Zen tradition, called this shift the "backward step." In Dogen's famous formulation, "body and mind fall away," as do views, opinions, and attachments, returning the practitioner to a state of open awareness. By putting his bag down, Hotei demonstrates an understanding of this process.

By picking his bag up again, however, Hotei enacts a complementary aspect of the practice, namely the reentry of the enlightened practitioner into ordinary life. Hotei is a wandering penniless monk, who has fully accepted the realities of impermanence and radical uncertainty. By once again shouldering his bag, he resumes his role in life and his life's work, which consists of helping people in general and children in particular be a little happier. In the language of Mahayana Buddhism, Hotei is a *bodhisattva*, who brings the mind of wisdom and compassion into the messy, uncertain, ordinary world. By picking up his bag, he becomes who he is, and he gets on with his work.

But why is he laughing? What's so funny? In his article "The Laughing Buddha and Human Pomposity," Dr. Philip Woollcott suggests that the celebration of Hotei and the "boisterous Zen humor" he represents came about as a healthy reaction to pious dogma and a calcified religious bureaucracy. "Enlightenment," Dr. Woollcott notes, "is the burning up of ego, the release from self-deception, and a new beginning; hence its connection with the child." All too often, however, the experience of enlightenment leads to self-importance and grandiosity. The presence of the Laughing Buddha subverts "hierarchy and pomp." It "collapses hierarchies and separateness among people." In contrast to scornful or supercilious laughter, a good belly laugh is a "sign of sanity." It rejoins us with the human family.

Perhaps that's why Allegra's spontaneous, volcanic laughter was such a delight and wonder to behold. A moment of Zen, one might be tempted to call it, had Jon Stewart not patented the phrase.

5 December 2013

A Space for Contemplation

Four weeks ago, in anticipation of the fiftieth anniversary of John F. Kennedy's assassination, we of a certain age were asked to recall where we were when the president was shot. As it happened, I was then a sophomore at Drake University in Des Moines, Iowa, and I listened to the announcement of the president's death in the lobby of Goodwin-Kirk Residence Hall, where a few of us had gathered around a portable radio. In retrospect, however, the question of where I was seems less important than where I went, having just received that sad and shocking news.

Drake University was founded in 1881. The school was originally affiliated with the Disciples of Christ Church, but since the 1950s the architectural tone of Drake's secular campus has been set by nine buildings designed by Eliel Saarinen and his son, Eero. In lieu of ivy and Roman columns, these buildings feature metal, brick, and glass, and they evoke the spirit of postwar industrial progress. Amidst these modern, rectilinear forms stands the university chapel, a round, brick-faced building designed by Eero Saarinen and dedicated in November 1955. Known as the Oreon E. Scott Memorial Chapel and situated near the center of the campus, this short, cylindrical form seems both starkly incongruous and oddly consistent with the neighboring buildings. Windowless and unadorned, it resembles an abbreviated silo.

Stepping inside, however, the visitor encounters an interior as rare as it is minimal: a darkened, intimate, and silent space, lit only by natural light. At the center of that space stands a circular communion table, four feet in diameter, its white marble made luminous by a central oculus in the ceiling. From the table's light-reflecting center, concentric rings of gray slate steps flow out to a circular prayer rail. Behind the rail, twenty straight, high-backed chairs circumscribe the inner space. Behind the chairs, a wood-slatted circular wall imparts a measure of warmth to an otherwise cool interior.

It was to this space that I went on the afternoon of November 22, 1963. When the heavy wooden doors closed behind me, I found myself in subdued light and utterly alone. Like millions of others, I had just incurred a trauma, and for the next hour or so I coped with it as best I could, aided and sheltered by my surroundings. I wrote a few lines of verse, which I would later discard. But for the most part I sat in solitude and silence, allowing my turbulent thoughts and my feelings of sadness, shock, and fear to settle in my awareness. "There is great beauty and peace," wrote the monk Thomas Merton in his journal, "in this life of silence and emptiness." Secluded from the violent and newly unstable world outside, I felt that silence and that emptiness, and they steadied my heart and mind.

At the same time, however, the silence and solitude of the chapel brought me face to face with what had happened, a few hours earlier, in Dealey Plaza. "Solitude is a stern mother," Merton also wrote in his journal, "who brooks no nonsense." And the Scott Memorial Chapel, for all its midcentury, minimalist beauty, offered no soothing platitudes or comforting icons—no Good Shepherd or Mother Mary, or Lord Buddha for that matter. Quite the opposite: the chapel's austere, egalitarian ambience, its whites, grays, browns, and blacks, encouraged an unmitigated encounter, free of distractions, with the reality of the present moment. Although I had yet to witness the moving pageantry of the funeral cortege or endure the commentary and speculation that continue to this day, I was, in Merton's phrase, "in perfect touch with reality." However naive I might been, politically and historically, I knew that something momentous, indeed tectonic, had just occurred. And that salutary realism, enforced by my environment, helped me maintain my equanimity.

In his general design, and in keeping with a theme of connectedness, Eero Saarinen created a covered walkway between the Scott Chapel and the adjacent Medbury Hall, which then housed the School of Divinity. That school closed in 1968, and Medbury now houses the Honors Program and the Department of Philosophy and Religion. But the Scott Chapel remains, much as it was in 1963, and it is now an unaffiliated, non-sectarian space, where visitors of all faiths—or none—can meditate, contemplate, or pray, according to their lights. I am happy to report that in 2007 Drake University had the wisdom to renovate the chapel's disintegrating fabric and restore it to its former distinction. Truth to tell, I do not know where else I would have gone.

19 December 2013

The Steady Go of the World

Twelve years ago, my wife and I planted a row of Red Twig Dogwoods on the western border of our back yard. They are now more than twelve feet tall. As I look out on this cold winter morning, I notice again how the dogwoods' deep-red branches contrast with the prevailing whites, grays, and browns. Against a dormant and seemingly lifeless landscape, they remind us of the life force.

The poet Gerard Manley Hopkins called that force "the dearest freshness deep down things." Dylan Thomas called it "the force that through the green fuse drives the flower." More simply, the Zen teacher Shohaku Okumura, in his book *Living by Vow*, calls it the "natural universal life force," which appears most vividly in nature but is common to the natural and human worlds alike. "The force that drives the water through the rock," Thomas went on to say, "drives my red blood." "We are all connected," writes Okumura, "one universal life force."

The connection to which Okumura alludes is readily verified, but in our everyday lives we may easily lose sight of it. And one of the primary aims of sitting meditation is to reconnect us with the life force within and around us. "We start right from this posture in silence," Okumura explains, "from the ever-fresh life force that is free from any defilement." And as we sit in silence, we "seek to manifest the universal life force which we have been given. We live on this earth with everything we need as a gift from nature." Merely by sitting still, we can become aware of that boundless gift, and we can also seek to "live out" the life force, allowing it "to practice *through* us for all living beings."

Known in Zen as "just sitting," this practice is simple but not always easy. It requires us to sit absolutely still and attend to whatever is occurring, within and around us. But should we commit ourselves to the practice, we may come to see how everything is changing, moment by moment, and how embodiments of the life force persist and grow, even as they negate themselves. A seed becomes a shoot, a shoot a flower. An infant becomes a child. When we seek to control the life force, Okumura warns, we diminish it. But if we put our wholehearted energies into the present moment, allowing the life force to manifest within us, its fruits will grow naturally. "We think our life is a failure and that we're in trouble. But the life force is flexible. There is always some other way to live, to grow, and to manifest our life force."

Many things can hinder our living out the life force, chief among them our inner chatter and our habits of excessive thinking. But as Okumura elsewhere reminds us, part of our life force is our power of thought. And, as the poet Seamus Heaney demonstrates in his poem "Perch," the practice of contemplation, supported by language, thought, and poetic form, can bring us close to that "freshness deep down things."

A ten-line poem consisting of a single sentence, "Perch" recalls Heaney's observation of those small freshwater fish in the Bann River in County Derry:

Perch on their water-perch hung in the clear Bann River
Near the clay bank in alder-dapple and waver,

Perch we called "grunts," little flood-snubs, runty and ready,
I saw and I see in the river's glorified body

That is passable through, but they're bluntly holding the pass,
Under the water-roof, over the bottom, adoze,

Guzzling the current, against it, all muscle and slur
In the finland of perch, the fenland of alder, on air

That is water, on carpets of Bann stream, on hold
In the everything flows and steady go of the world.

In this brief, intimate lyric, Heaney observes a balance of movement and stasis in the natural world. An imagery of incessant activity—the alders' reflections, the river's current—is countered by an image of stability: the dozing perch, suspended between the "river-roof" and the river's bottom. And, like the perch "holding the pass," the poem's off-rhymed couplets (*river/waver; ready/body*) create a succession of fixed but permeable forms, through which the long, sinuous sentence flows. In the presence of these balanced forces, natural and literary, the narrator summons a fondly remembered experience to present awareness.

"Zen and poetry are one," an old Zen saying tells us. In this instance, Heaney's poem enacts a moment in which the life force co-exists harmoniously with contemplative thought. Vested with the power of thought, the narrator contemplates the life force. Held by thought to a single point, he experiences—and honors—the "steady go of the world."

6 February 2014

This

"Support for NPR," announced National Public Radio's Sabrina Farhi during the holiday season, "comes from Pajamagram, makers of matching holiday pajamas for the whole family, including dogs and cats." After listing several other sponsors, Ms. Farhi concluded with a single declarative sentence: *"This . . .* (pause)," said she, "is NPR." She might have been delivering a dramatic monologue, so pronounced was her emphasis on *this* and so protracted the ensuing pause.

Ms. Farhi has since abandoned that mannerism, but its temporary recurrence on *Morning Edition,* morning after morning, brought to mind the prominence of the word *this,* similarly isolated, in the Zen tradition. Generally speaking, in Zen practice *this* refers to undifferentiated reality, prior to the imposition of conceptual thought. "Just this," a phrase familiar to Zen students, is what we experience when we penetrate the filter created by dualistic concepts, particularly such ego-centered dualities as "self/other," "I/they," and "mine/

not mine." To remain in continuous contact with *this*, while also questioning its nature, is central to Zen practice. And to lose touch with or misconstrue the nature of *this* is likely to bring suffering upon oneself and others.

In the Vietnamese tradition of Rinzai Zen, as interpreted by the Venerable Thich Nhat Hanh, apprehension of *this* begins with the cultivation of mindfulness (*sati*), which Thich Nhat Hanh defines as being present for the present moment. According to classical Buddhist teachings, we can bring mindfulness to any one of four general fields, or "foundations," of awareness: the body, the feelings, the mind, or "objects of mind." If we are practicing systematically, we may choose which of these fields we wish to be mindful of, and in what order. If not, we can merely direct our attention to whatever phenomena might arise, moving gently from one to another. What is important is to be present, fully and consciously, whether the object of mindfulness be random or systematically chosen.

Continuous mindfulness concentrates the mind. In Thich Nhat Hanh's words, "[t]he energy of mindfulness carries within it the energy of concentration," and the two energies work in tandem. When our capacity to be continuously aware has grown strong enough, we can shift our orientation from the practice of mindfulness to the practice of concentration (*samadhi*), which is based on mindful awareness but differs in several ways. Where mindfulness is inclusive, concentration is exclusive. It isolates a specific object—one component, as it were, of *this*—and gives that object sustained, uninterrupted attention. And where mindfulness exemplifies "effortless effort," concentration requires a conscious act of will. In Zen teachings, mindfulness is sometimes likened to a lamp, which illuminates the mind. Concentration resembles a spotlight, which the practitioner trains on a particular object.

If, for example, you are practicing mindfulness of your mental states, and you realize you are angry, you can shine that spotlight on your anger. Maintaining your focus on that feeling, you may discern that its immediate cause is a vicious insult vividly remembered. You can still see the speaker's face and hear his hurtful words. By bringing the energy of concentration to bear upon that incident, you can investigate the causes and conditions which brought it about. At the same time, by remaining mindful of your breathing, your bodily sensations, and your present state of mind, you can protect yourself from merely reliving a painful experience.

Should you succeed in this effort, you will have entered the third dimension of the practice, namely that of insight (*prajna*). Looking more deeply into the remembered incident, you may come to realize that your verbal assailant was himself distressed, and though you were the object of his attack, you were not necessarily its cause. Concurrently, you may also recognize your own role, however limited or unintentional, in provoking the attack. And, most centrally, you may come to see that your present mental state, however solid it may feel, is in reality no more substantial than a passing cloud. In an hour it may be gone. Acknowledging its impermanent nature, you can begin to release yourself from its grip. And over time, if you persist in the practice, the roots of the feeling may disappear altogether.

"What is this?" asked the Zen master Bassui Tokusho (1327–1387), enjoining us to pose that question over and again, whether *this* be an orange, a thought, or a state of mind. Through the practice outlined above, adapted to suit our personal circumstances, we can pursue Bassui's question, not as an abstract philosophical inquiry but as a means toward stability, clarity of mind, and eventual liberation. And we can learn to live more wisely.

27 February 2014

Well-met in Belfast

"*F*or Ben Howard, well met in Belfast, July, 2004."

So wrote a gentlemanly Irish poet, whose work I had long admired, in the flyleaf of his most recent book. At the time, he and I were having lunch in the upstairs dining room of the Crown Liquor Saloon, a storied old pub in the heart of Belfast, Northern Ireland. I had come up on the train from Dublin to meet him.

Of the many inscriptions I have acquired over the years, few have proved as memorable as the one above, partly because the poet's chosen phrase, faintly archaic but resonantly apt, sorted well with the Crown's Victorian decor—its ornate tin ceilings, stained-glass windows, and dark-paneled "snugs." Regrettably, "well-met" is no longer current in North America, either as a description or a greeting. Once the equivalent of "Nice to have met you," that old-fashioned phrase evokes a singular event: two people meeting, in the fullness of human relationship, at a particular place and time.

"All real living is meeting," wrote the philosopher Martin Buber. And in his book *Taking Our Places*, an exploration of Zen practice as a path to maturity, the Zen priest Norman Fischer takes Buber's pronouncement as his abiding theme. Reflecting on Buber's words, Fischer recalls that when he thought hard about the "Zen enlightenment stories," he realized that they are "less about solitary visionary experience than the saving possibility of human relationship. . . . Enlightenment is the fruit not of isolation but of connection." When Buber said that all real living is meeting, he was making "the profound observation that when we truly meet one another . . . and open ourselves to each other with the courage to step toward one another, then and only then can we be said to be completely alive."

Fischer's point is well taken, but as he goes on to acknowledge, in the everyday world such meetings are infrequent. How often do any of us "truly meet one another"? And how can such encounters be engendered and supported?

To begin with, we might bear in mind the Japanese motto *ichigo ichie*, which is commonly translated as "one time, one meeting." Closely associated with the Zen tradition, *ichigo ichie* reminds us that every encounter, however familiar or habitual, is a once-in-a-lifetime experience. It is unprecedented and unrepeatable. To be sure, the "meeting" in question might seem as ordinary as having lunch with a friend or getting together after work for a drink. But because conditions are always changing, one's present experience is in reality unique. By reminding ourselves of that fact, we can cultivate an attitude of freshness toward each new encounter.

"Beginner's mind," as this attitude is known in Zen, is especially important as it pertains to the act of listening. Mary

Rose O'Reilley, a writer, college professor, and Zen practitioner, notes that in academic culture, "most listening is critical listening.... We mentally grade and pigeonhole each other." And in society at large, "people often listen with an agenda, to sell or petition or seduce." As a constructive alternative, O' Reilley advocates a "deep, openhearted, unjudging reception of the other." When she encounters such a reception, "[her] spirit begins to expand." And it is possible, she believes, to *"listen someone into existence*, encourage a stronger self to emerge or a new talent to flourish."

Norman Fischer shares O'Reilley's perspective, but he also believes that as listeners we have an obligation to respond. "We cannot only be passive listeners. In the end, listening's completion is *negotiation*." Toward that end, he recommends two techniques developed by the mediator Gary Friedman. The first is known as "looping" and consists of listening carefully and then repeating, as accurately as one can, what the other person has just said. In this way the "loop of communication" is completed. The second technique, known as "dipping," consists of pausing during a conversation to "check in with" our own thoughts and feelings. In this way, we take our present state of mind into account—and weigh our words accordingly. Together these two techniques, which Fischer has employed in social contexts as diverse as an employees' retreat at Yale University and a peace conference in Belfast, have sometimes yielded startling revelations. Participants in the Belfast conference, Fischer reports, were shocked to discover that they hadn't even been hearing one another, much less promoting peace.

Not every meeting can be so rewarding. Some must be purely professional, if proper boundaries are to be maintained. But as Fischer and O'Reilley remind us, and as their experiences confirm, it is possible to approach almost any meeting with full attention, an open heart, and an attitude of deep respect. More often than we might suppose, it is possible to be well-met.

20 March 2014

Lessons of the Selfie

Over the past few years the digital self-portrait has come into its own. Decried by some as a symptom of narcissism, celebrated by others as a vehicle of self-empowerment, the so-called "selfie" has assumed center stage, not only in social media but in the media at large. Ellen DeGeneres' "group selfie," spontaneously snapped at the Oscars, may well be the world's most widely viewed example, but it is literally one among millions.

In another decade or two, we may find out whether the selfie was a fad, a portent of a cultural shift, or something else entirely. But from the vantage point of Zen teachings, the ubiquitous selfie, shot in a mirror or from an outstretched hand, offers what is known as a "dharma gate": a point of entry into a deeper truth. "To study the way," wrote the thirteenth-century Zen master Eihei Dogen, "is to study the self." And the phenomenon of the selfie, however superficial it may seem, provides an opportunity to do just that.

To begin with, the selfie underscores, as never before, a fundamental quality of the self, namely its radical impermanence. Posed self-portraits on canvas have been with us for centuries, and their earliest photographic counterparts date from the late nineteenth century. But the digital self-portrait, taken, as it were, on the fly, represents something new, insofar as it is a transitory image of a transitory subject. It can be deleted, whether by accident or design, in an instant and at any time. Our most basic misperception, Buddhist teachings tell us, is "taking what is not self to be self." We mistake what Joseph Goldstein has called the "pairwise progression of subject and object, arising and passing moment after moment," for a lasting entity. We posit continuity where it may or may not exist, and we construct from successive moments the concept of an unchanging self. To that persistent habit of mind, the vulnerable digital image offers a potent corrective. It prompts us to inquire whether the self we assume to be solid and enduring may be no more substantial than the virtual image on our screens.

Even as it demonstrates the impermanence of the self, however, the selfie may also challenge our conventional notion of the life span: the personal self's finite existence. As many users of social media have discovered to their chagrin, self-portraits posted on the Internet can last far beyond their creators' original intention. Their life spans, if such exist, are not always in our control. According to the *Diamond Sutra*, a fundamental text of the Zen tradition, the concept of a life span is itself an erroneous notion and a primary source of human suffering. "A cloud can never die," writes Zen master Thich Nhat Hanh. "It can only become rain or snow." Nothing is annihilated, only transformed. And what is true of the cloud, the *Diamond Sutra* asserts, is also true of ourselves. Whether as stardust, a field of energy, a photo on a dresser, or an impression in a loved one's memory bank, we continue beyond our dates of expiration. The enduring digital image, launched into cyberspace and winding up who knows where, can alert us to that eventuality—and prompt us to act accordingly.

Yet, lest the lessons of the selfie be restricted to the personal, it is worth remembering that the digital self-image also represents the interdependent nature of the conditioned self. The one includes the whole. However conformist or individualistic, conventional or outlandish any one selfie might be, its very existence exemplifies what the Zen priest Shohaku Okumura has called the "network of interdependent origination." More concretely, it represents a complex network, at once electronic, social, and economic, whose components include the makers of micro-chips and smart phones, the creators and managers of social media, the purveyors of laptops, desktops, and mobile devices, and the eager consumers of such products. For all its elevation of the affluent leisured self, the selfie offers a context in which to contemplate something beyond the self: the one, indivisible body of interconnected reality.

"To study the self," Dogen went on to say, "is to forget the self; and to forget the self is to be enlightened by the ten thousand things." Viewing a recent selfie, which features a muscular young man flexing his bicep in the mirror, I suspect that the enlightenment of which Dogen speaks may not be high among the photographer's priorities. But it remains an ever-present possibility, whether its vehicle be a cup of tea, an ephemeral mandala, or yet another selfie.

3 April 2014

Call It a Notion

We can throw away a soiled tissue. We can throw away Q-tips, outdated appliances, and countless other items in our everyday lives. But can we also discard our ill-founded thoughts and one-sided perceptions? Our cherished notions?

According to classical Buddhist teachings, many if not most of our perceptions are erroneous, and erroneous perceptions cause suffering. "Looking deeply into the wrong perceptions, ideas, and notions that are at the base of our suffering," writes Zen master Thich Nhat Hanh, "is the most important practice in Buddhist meditation." And correspondingly, "the practice of throwing away your notions and views is so important. Liberation will not be possible without this throwing away." Yet, as Thich Nhat Hanh goes on to say, "it takes insight and courage to throw away an idea." Views we have held for decades—or perhaps for a lifetime—are not so easily disposed of, especially when they appear to have served us well.

Broadly speaking, one of the most effective ways to rid ourselves of self-centered, noxious views, such as the view that one's own race, gender, class, or ethnicity is superior to another, is to reflect deeply on that view's potential for harm. But a more immediate tool resides in one of the words Thich Nhat Hanh employs above. That word is *notion*, which has multiple meanings within a distinctive tonal range. Most commonly, *notion* refers to an idea, view, or concept, but it may also refer to a whim, a hunch, an intuition, or an impulse. In Ireland, *notion* can mean an inflated sense of one's importance, social status, or charm. ("She has notions, that one. She thinks she's it"). Similarly, in American usage *notion* is often paired with *fanciful*, suggesting that the notion in question may be imaginative but not well grounded in fact.

As these diverse meanings indicate, calling a thought a notion is not quite the same as calling it an idea or view, much less a firm belief or bedrock conviction. The very word notion implies that the connection between the thought and the reality it purports to represent might be tenuous at best. Where before there was certainty, now there is doubt. Where once we believed our own thought, now we are not so sure. And from the vantage point of meditative practice, that is a fortunate situation in which to find ourselves.

For one thing, viewing our thoughts as notions encourages us to step back from them, rather than identify with them or automatically assume their validity. As Joseph Goldstein reminds us, there is a "profound difference between being aware of a thought and being lost in it." By becoming aware of a thought even as it is arising, we prevent ourselves from getting lost in it, attached to it, or anchored in it prematurely. And by viewing it as merely a notion, we can more readily see what Goldstein calls its "changing, selfless nature." Should we find the thought worth pursuing, we can do so at a later time. If not, we can witness the thought's arrival, duration, and departure and allow it to disappear of its own accord.

Reciprocally, by regarding a thought as a transient, insubstantial notion, we can also drain it of much of its power. "A thought is just a thought," the Burmese meditation master Sayada U Tejaniya observes. But thoughts about matters that deeply concern us—our health, finances, jobs, and families, to name a few—can dominate our minds and erode our equanimity, whether they be grounded in reality or not. By viewing our thoughts as notions, we can learn to give our views and ideas a fair hearing but not take them all that seriously or attribute importance where none exists. The Tibetan master Sogyal Rinpoche advises us to view our "family of thoughts" as children at play. Zen master Koshu Uchiyama urges us to see them as the mind's "secretions." Similarly, by viewing even our brightest thoughts as notions, we can release ourselves from their grip.

Should we succeed in that effort, we will have opened a meditative space where our thoughts no longer undermine the clarity of our seeing or diminish our appreciation of our daily lives. Thich Nhat Hanh notes that the word *nirvana* originally meant (among other things) "the extinction of all notions." Given the profusion of thoughts that can cross our minds in an hour's time, the extinction of even one pernicious thought may seem a lofty aspiration. But we can start by becoming fully aware that we are *having* that thought—and by calling it a notion.

8 May 2014

Making Whole

"Do not lose yourself in the future," Buddhist teachings advise. "Look deeply at life as it is in this very moment." Under most circumstances that is sound advice, but it can also be devilishly difficult to follow. It is human nature to dwell on the future, especially when the future is replete with uncertainties.

So it was not long ago, when I learned that I needed minor surgery, and I met with my surgeon for a pre-op consultation. A seasoned professional in his sixties, he explained the nature of the procedure, including its history and technical details, and outlined the stages of recovery. During the first week, I would be laid up and managing pain, but by the second I would probably be feeling "fifty percent better." By the end of the third, I might well be free of pain, though patients sometimes report "nuisance discomfort." Six to eight weeks out, I would probably be able to resume my customary activities.

That forecast was reassuring, but by their nature forecasts focus on the future, and they leave open the question of what the patient, his eyes on the horizon, should be doing in the meantime. In a recent article (*Prevention*, January 2014), Sister Dang Nghiem, MD, a Western-trained physician and a Buddhist nun, offers this prescription:

> *It's a myth to say that time can heal. Time cannot heal. Breathing and mindfulness can. [Long after a traumatic event happens to you], a sight, a sound, a smell, a taste, a touch can trigger the complete stress response as though it's happening all over again . . . Through breathing, you learn to slow the stress response, the fight-flight-or-freeze response. If you can do that when going through a very intense experience, the next time you recall that trauma, you will do so with more peace, mindfulness, and clarity.*

Here Sister Dang is speaking of emotional trauma, but her reflections also apply to such physical traumas as surgery. Mindful breathing calms the body and steadies the mind. For many people, the practice of mindfulness has proved helpful in managing pain and promoting the process of healing.

Yet it would be a mistake to presume that mindfulness alone can eliminate pain or cure a serious illness. And in any event, as the Zen teacher Roshi Pat Enkyo O'Hara reminds us, meditative practice has more than comfort to offer the injured, sick, and dying. In her book *Most Intimate: A Zen Approach to Life's Challenges*, Roshi O'Hara notes that the root meaning of the word healing is "making whole." And in compelling detail, she recounts her experience of a painful and protracted illness, which robbed her of her strength and plunged her into chronic depression. Her loss of strength in particular unnerved her, because she had always thought of herself as strong and energetic. Disabled by her condition and depressed by her medication, she felt less than whole.

All of that changed, however, when Roshi O'Hara realized that by clinging to an idea of her former physical condition as "whole" and her present one as something less, she was turning away from the reality of her illness. She was rejecting the totality of her experience. And by viewing her pain and weakness as enemies, she was also denying herself the very medicine that could help her heal:

> *Can we remember that pain and weakness and death are not our enemies. . . . That it is our fear and rejection of pain and weakness and death that are our enemies? That it is that rejection, that casting out, that incapacitates us and does not allow us to live life with courage and fearlessness?*

By no longer viewing her illness as her enemy, Roshi O'Hara came to see herself as whole, despite the pain in her joints and the other symptoms of her illness. By training herself, breath by breath, to be present for all of her experience, including her pain and fatigue, she supported the process of healing, while also addressing the root of her suffering. "Even when we are ill," she observes, "we are wholly and completely who we are . . . What needs to be healed is our idea that we are not whole at this moment."

After a long course of treatment, Roshi O'Hara recovered. She regained her strength. Although she does not attribute her recovery solely to her meditative practice, it is clear that her "medicine" helped her endure the process of recovery and healing. And in telling her story, she offers a valuable perspective, not only for dealing with infirmity but also for meeting the world.

5 June 2014

Anything Can Happen Anytime

For more than four decades Joseph Goldstein, an internationally known teacher of Buddhist meditation, has practiced mindfulness of the body and mind. First as a monk in the Thai forest tradition and later as a Western practitioner, he has trained himself to be aware of what is occurring, within and without, in any given moment. Yet one afternoon, while walking along a river in northern New Mexico, Goldstein slipped on a wet rock and hyper-extended his knee. At the time, he was conducting a retreat, and later on that day, after giving a talk in the cross-legged position, he found himself unable to stand or walk. For the next few hours he berated himself and worried that he would not be able to complete the retreat. But in the midst of his anguish, he reports, a "sort of mantra" arose in his mind: *Anything can happen anytime.* To his surprise, that "mantra" provided a great sense of relief. Since then, he has found it "amazingly helpful in accepting change with a deepening and easeful equanimity."

If you are of a skeptical nature, you may be wondering how a simple declarative sentence—and that sentence in particular—could have so powerful an impact. Anything can happen anytime? Taken as a general proposition, that statement is demonstrably untrue. Pigs can't fly and never will; the elbow does not bend outward. But even if the sentence is understood as a functional slogan rather than a literal truth, it might as easily be heard as a warning or a sigh of resignation or even a cry of despair. Why should it bring a sense of relief, much less a deepening sense of balance and peace?

One answer is that the realization that "anything can happen anytime" shifts our orientation from the needs, expectations, and other aspects of the self to the impersonal causes and conditions underlying a particular event. When things go awry, it is all too easy to view one's own actions—or someone else's—as the sole or principal cause. In reality, however, most occurrences have multiple causes, and one's own role, however large or small, conscious or unintentional, is only a part of the picture. External conditions—the weather, the time of day, the physical environment—may play as large or larger a part. To realize as much can lift a heavy and often misplaced burden of responsibility from our hearts and minds.

By the same token, the recognition that "anything can happen anytime" can free us from the illusion of personal control. As Goldstein puts it, his mantra is a reminder that "yes, this is how things are. Conditions are always changing and often outside our control. We don't have to live defensively if we accept that anything can happen anytime." Insofar as we struggle to control what cannot be controlled, we suffer. And insofar as we imagine ourselves to be fully in charge of what happens in our lives, we live in delusion and denial. By summoning Goldstein's mantra, or allowing it to arise of its own accord, we can restore our realism and our sense of proportion.

At a deeper level, Goldstein's mantra can also put us in touch with what Zen teachings call *sunyata*—a Sanskrit term variously translated as "emptiness," "nothingness," and "absolute reality." *Sunyata* refers to the vast, interdependent network of changing causes and conditions, of which any one "thing" or event is a fluid part. The one includes the all. By reminding ourselves that anything can happen anytime, we also remind ourselves of *sunyata*, where energies are constantly being exchanged, where "this is, because that is," and where, in an instant, what we thought was solid and enduring can disappear or become something else. Far from describing a void, the term *sunyata* evokes a field of radical impermanence and infinite possibility. And to contemplate *sunyata* is, in the fullness of time, to free ourselves from attachment to "things," the past, and self-centered views.

To be sure, Goldstein's mantra may not be enough to release us from the anxieties, doubts, and fears that many of us entertain in our dreams and carry with us into our waking hours. Those mental pollutants are not so readily expunged. But "anything can happen anytime" may well help us to accept what Zen teachings call the "vicissitudes"—the ups and downs of gain and loss, praise and blame, health and infirmity, joy and pain. Evoked in times of stress, this resonant reminder can help us live with grace and equanimity in a world where things are seldom stable or certain, our paths are sometimes slippery, and anything can happen anytime.

3 July 2014

Let's Not Go There

In his poignant essay "The Old Order," the Irish-American writer James Silas Rogers recalls his conversation on an Amtrak train with a young Amish man named Johann, who was crossing Wisconsin with his extended family. Curious about Amish faith and belief, Rogers inquired as to the significance of Johann's distinctive attire: his plain shirt, suspenders, and broadfall trousers. "People ask us," Johann replied, "if we think that wearing these clothes will get us into heaven. We absolutely do not.... But I do know that if I wear these clothes, it will keep me out of places where I should not go."

Reading Johann's explanation, I was reminded of formal Zen practice, which also employs special clothes to remind practitioners of their moral commitments. In Japanese Zen, one of the most conspicuous of those clothes is the *rakusu*, a bib-like garment worn (and often hand-sewn) by those who have "taken the precepts," which is to say, have publicly affirmed a set of ethical guidelines. Known as the "*jukai* precepts," those guidelines differ from sect to sect, but in essence they enjoin the Zen disciple to refrain from harmful behaviors, particularly killing, stealing, engaging in false or injurious speech, using sexuality in hurtful ways, and abusing intoxicants. The unadorned rakusu, viewed as a miniature monastic robe and inscribed on the back with its wearer's "dharma name," signifies a commitment to that fundamental code of conduct.

In Zen practice, ethical behavior is inextricable from present awareness. Each supports the other. Correspondingly, the rakusu is not only a reminder of the precepts but also a symbol of a quality of mind, namely that of continuous, wholehearted mindfulness. In its secular applications, mindfulness is sometimes equated with heightened sensory awareness—being fully present for the present moment. But in its deeper, monastic context, the practice of mindfulness also embodies a moral dimension. Truly to be mindful is to remember the precepts and one's best intentions in every thought, word, and deed. By so doing, we live in harmony with things as they are, and we avoid doing harm to others and ourselves.

In his book *Training in Compassion*, the Zen teacher Zoketsu Norman Fischer explains concretely how training in mindfulness can forestall harmful behavior. Focusing on our "default habits," those "unsuccessful yet compelling attitudes, thoughts, and actions that seem to keep coming back, over and over again, despite our best intentions," Fischer identifies three "difficulties" associated with changing destructive habits of mind.

The first difficulty is to recognize the habitual impulse whenever it arises. The second is to let go of the mental habit, however compelling or gratifying it might be. And the third is to let go of the habit yet again, the next time it arises. This can be especially difficult because of the "habit energy" that has driven the thought or attitude or action, perhaps for a lifetime.

But how, exactly, is one to "let go" of ingrained patterns of thought and action? Broadly speaking, Fischer recommends two methods, the first to be employed during sitting meditation and the second to practice in everyday life. The first consists of recognizing unwholesome states of mind arising, and upon doing so, returning to "the feeling of the breath and the body." By practicing in this way, we become aware of such states as anger, fear, and jealousy at their moment of inception. By returning to the breath and body, we decline to nourish those unwholesome states.

The second method consists of this "three-step program":

Step 1: notice when habitual negative thinking arises. Step 2: stop. Literally stop for a moment: if you are walking, stop walking; if you are sitting, stand up; if you are thinking, stop thinking. Step 3: take a breath. Return to awareness with that breath. This simple three-step practice is surprisingly powerful. . . .

In presenting this practice as a three-part formula, Fischer does not minimize its complexities. On the contrary, he acknowledges that "mostly the training will proceed from failure to failure." But by stopping, taking a breath, and "then with that breath returning to positive intentions," the practitioner can gradually replace harmful habits of mind with beneficial ones, while also gaining strength in the practice.

"Let's not go there," my wife sometimes cautions, when our conversations drift toward some painful episode from the past, or I express a negative, all-too-familiar view. Like Johann's broadfall trousers, her admonition reminds me to be aware of persistent, corrosive habits of thought and feeling, even as they are arising. Whether I or anyone can internalize that external voice, however, and heed it when appropriate, is quite another matter. An aspiration worthy of concerted effort, it is also a formidable challenge of meditative practice.

14 August 2014

Yeah, Whatever

"I think most people would lie to get ahead."

"It is safer to trust nobody."

"Most people will use somewhat unfair reasons to gain profit or an advantage rather than lose it."

If you would tend to agree with those statements, your outlook on life and human nature might fairly be described as one of cynical distrust. And while you might be well established in that outlook—and even take pride in being a curmudgeon—a recent Finnish study might give you pause.

Sponsored by the University of Eastern Finland, this study of 1449 subjects with an average age of 71 found a striking correlation between high degrees of cynical distrust and subsequent incidences of senile dementia. Those who looked at the world though cynical eyes, the researchers discovered, were three times as likely to develop dementia than those who did not. "If that's really true," a friend in his sixties quipped, "I'm going to be babbling any day now."

To be sure, the Finnish study has yet to be replicated, and it only demonstrated a correlation, not a cause-and-effect relationship. But whatever its validity, this disturbing study might prompt us to examine elements of cynicism in our own outlooks—and, if we so wish, to cultivate a counterbalancing alternative. And toward those ends, the practice of Zen meditation has something substantial to offer.

When we practice *zazen* (sitting meditation), we sit in an aligned, relaxed, and resilient posture. Bringing our attention to our breathing, we feel the life force within and around us. Depending on our method, we may choose to count our breaths, recite a mantra, explore a koan, or merely rest in "choiceless awareness." If our mind drifts into worries and dreams, we bring it back to our breath. If we begin to slouch, we correct our posture. After ten, fifteen, or twenty minutes of this practice, we may notice that our breathing has deepened and our minds feel clearer. In classical Zen teachings, this process is likened to mud settling to the bottom of a jar, leaving the water still and clear.

Should we direct this poised clarity of awareness toward the external world, we may find that our vision of the day's events, global, national, and local, has also become more balanced, impartial, and inclusive. Reading or watching the news, we are likely to encounter reports of petty and large-scale violence, corruption, greed, exploitation, and inhumanity generally. Far from shielding us from those social realities, the practice of meditation may make us more aware than ever of what Zen teachings call the "three poisons" of craving, aversion, and ignorance and the suffering they engender. But by deepening our outlook, meditative practice can also make us acutely aware of the complexity of human motives, which include not only greed and hatred but also loving-kindness, compassion, sympathetic joy, and the desire to relieve others' suffering. Resolved to "welcome everything" into our awareness, while putting our preferences in abeyance, we may be less inclined to reduce the human condition to a single, cynical view.

By the same token, if we bring a balanced awareness to our inner lives, we might discern a complex amalgam of thoughts, feelings, motives, and habits of mind. If one of those components is an habitual cynical distrust, we might look into what the Venerable Thich Nhat Hanh calls the "roots and fruits" of that attitude. Snide comments and cynical posturing can be entertaining and win us social approval. Could a desire to entertain or gain social acceptance underlie our expressions of cynical scorn? Or might their origin lie in our life experience—in some deep hurt or emotional trauma, which our cynicism serves to mask? Merely by bringing awareness to the roots of habitual cynicism, we can mitigate its power. And even as we examine the foundations of cynical distrust, we can also contemplate its "fruits": its probable effects on our own lives and those with whom we come into contact. If we habitually say "Yeah, right" to any sentiment that expresses optimism, or hints at a vulnerable naivete, what impact is our attitude having on our fellow workers? Our friends and family? Our children and grandchildren? And what, in the long run, is its legacy likely to be?

Cynicism is sometimes viewed as the obverse side of moral idealism. Idealists, as they age, become bitter and caustic cynics. In contrast to other aspects of the aging process, however, such a change is not inevitable. If a cynical outlook is harmful to ourselves and others, why cherish or nourish it? With the help of meditative practice, there are changes we can make, and salutary things we can do.

11 September 2014

Put It in Neutral

"Put it in neutral, Bud," my father said, quietly but firmly. It was the summer of 1958, and I was learning to drive. The car was a 1950 Chevrolet sedan with a three-speed transmission and the gearshift lever on the steering column. "Three on the Tree," it was called. Learning to put the lever and the Chevy itself into neutral was my first lesson.

It might also be the first lesson for the Zen practitioner. Wherever else it might lead, the practice of Zen meditation begins with finding, establishing, and maintaining a neutral center, both for the body and the mind. Neutrality may well be the body-mind's most natural condition, but for many people it is far from habitual. In a culture as competitive as ours, neutrality is often not an option, much less a state to be cultivated and explored. To do so requires training and sustained attention.

The posture of meditation is a good place to start. Generally speaking, that posture should be upright, aligned, and resilient, whether one is sitting on a cushion, bench, or chair.

Even when we are sitting upright, however, the parts of our bodies may or may not be in a neutral state. That is why the standard instructions for Zen meditation direct us to rock in an arc from side to side and backward and forward until we find our neutral center. Once we have done so, we can then check the positions of the spine (upright, but following its natural curvature), wrists (gently curved, not angled), shoulders (neither slouched nor stiffly pulled back), head (chin tucked in; head not tilted up or down), eyes (neither closed nor wholly open), and other parts of our bodies. As the last step in this process, we can determine whether our general physical state, which in Zen teachings is likened to a lute string, is neither too tight nor too loose but at a neutral point in between.

As with the body, so with the mind. Here is how Zen teacher Jan Chozen Bays describes the state of mental neutrality, as experienced in *zazen* (sitting meditation):

> In zazen, the restless activity that separates us from everything-that-is settles. Boundaries dissolve and we become light and transparent, completely receptive. Heart and mind become clear and open. Then each breath is the sacred, original breath, moving across the face of the earth. Sound, light, and touch are the play of existence arising endlessly out of emptiness. There is nothing lacking, nothing to ask for—except that everyone else be able to experience this perfect ease.

In this neutral, non-judgmental sate, Bays goes on to say, we become aware of "the continual gift, of the outpouring of all that exists, from the bottomless font of the unknowable."

The state of mind which Jan Bays is describing (and which she likens to prayer) is that of an experienced Zen practitioner. A beginner's experience might be very different, as might that of even a seasoned practitioner on any given day. As anyone who undertakes this practice will soon discover, obstacles abound. From early childhood we are conditioned to be active and productive. Resting in awareness is easily perceived, even by ourselves, as laziness or a culpable passivity. As a result, both body and mind resist the neutral state. They want to be *doing* something. They want to *accomplish* something. And most of all, they want to be *gaining* something, whether it be immediate release from stress or eventual enlightenment. Merely to sit in a neutral, attentive state, aware of "everything-that-is" and open to it all, is a discipline to be acquired and a skill to be practiced. For many people, especially at the beginning, the state of neutrality can prove as elusive as it is beneficial.

All the same, anyone with the will to do so may experience a taste of this liberating and restorative practice. If you would like to try it, may I suggest that you choose an habitual activity—something as routine as reading your e-mail or making breakfast or cleaning your kitchen counter. In the midst of that activity, stop. Return to your breath and your body, allowing your engines, as it were, to idle. Observe the immediate effect on your senses, your feelings, and your state of mind. After a period of a minute or two, resume your normal activity, noting any changes in your attitude, your distance from or intimacy with your surroundings, and your performance of the task at hand. Continue this practice several times a day for at least a week, and observe its impact on your daily life.

9 September 2014

Not Two, Not One

"Up!" implores my granddaughter, looking up at me and raising her arms. Allegra is fifteen months old. *Up* was one of her first words.

I gladly pick Allegra up, and for the next few minutes I take her for a walk on my shoulder, making rhythmic noises in her ear. This seems to please her, but eventually she decides that she has indulged her grandfather long enough. "Down," says she, and I reluctantly comply.

Up and down, down and up. Over the next year and beyond, Allegra will learn other pairs of words and other dualities: left and right, inside and outside, high and low. Through the medium of language she will learn not only to speak but also to think in dualistic terms. Soon enough, I suspect, she will enlist the duality *yours* and *mine*, with a pronounced emphasis on the latter.

As do we grown-ups, every day of the year. Dualistic thinking is so familiar and so necessary for navigating the world, it goes unnoticed and unexamined much of the time.

Yet, as the Zen master Thich Nhat Hanh observes, our familiar dualities are relative in nature and impede our apprehension of reality:

> *Concepts such as high and low, one and many, coming and going, birth and death, are all important in everyday life. But when we leave the realm of the practical to meditate on the true nature of the universe, we must also leave behind these concepts. For example, when you raise your eyes to look up at the stars and moon, you say that they are "above." But at the very same moment, for someone standing on the opposite side of the planet, the direction you are looking is "below" for them. When looking at the entire universe, we have to abandon all these concepts of high and low, and so forth.*

Abandon all such concepts? As Thich Nhat Hanh goes on to say, our "way of thinking and speaking makes it difficult to penetrate non-dualistic, non-discriminatory reality, a reality which cannot be contained in concepts."

Of all the dualities we employ for our survival, none is more fundamental than that of "self" and "other." We learn that duality early on and apply it ever after. At the same time, our ordinary concept of "self" is often narrowly defined, and from the vantage point of Zen teachings, it is largely illusory. Broadly speaking, we tend to think of our "self" as something solid or at least continuous from decade to decade. And because our personal experiences differ from those of other people, we tend to view ourselves as separate from everyone and everything else. Our culture of individualism fervently supports that view.

Yet reality teaches otherwise. If we take "the backward step that illuminates the self," as Zen master Eihei Dogen (1200-1253) enjoins us to do, what we are likely to observe is a swift-flowing stream of information, impressions, memories, judgments, opinions, fantasies, and other mental phenomena, from which we construct and defend a coherent "self." We may think of that construct as akin to a stone, but in reality it more resembles a whirlpool. And far from being separate, it co-exists in a dynamic, interdependent relationship with the web of life, natural and human. In her book *Mindfully Green*, the environmentalist Stephanie Kaza describes that relationship in this way:

> *Each of us reflects the day's weather and the mood in our household. We act from the legacy of our parents' values and the deeply familiar psychological habits of our families of origin. We speak from our knowledge of woods and streams or oceans and beaches. We offer an opinion as a member of a company or agency. Looking closely at our situation, it becomes obvious: we don't exist apart from these systems.*

Viewed in this light, the simple duality of self and other loses much of its meaning. Like any one part of our bodies, the so-called self possesses a recognizable identity, but it also co-exists in an ever-changing relationship with multiple systems and the one body of undifferentiated reality.

"The mind divides," Zen teachings tell us, "and the heart unites." Can we keep the mind and heart in balance, knowing that our true self is inseparable from the one, indivisible body of the world? Perhaps not all the time. But as an effort in that direction, we can remind ourselves that "self" and "other," in the language of Zen, are "not two, not one": two in conventional, relative terms, but one with respect to the unity of all life.

6 November 2014

Immovable Awareness

Here in the village of Alfred, New York, those of us who like to walk can often be found on the Alfred State College track. Situated on a high elevation, the track affords a panoramic view of the surrounding wooded hills. Designed though it was for athletic competition, the track is also an excellent venue for walking meditation.

On a windy day last summer, I took a walk on that firm but forgiving track. Above the line of trees, the blades of the college's wind turbine were revolving briskly. And on the tall flagpole near the entrance, the American flag was flapping audibly. I was reminded of an old Zen story, which features a pair of quarrelsome monks and the enlightened master Eno, the Sixth Patriarch of Zen.

In this story, the two monks are arguing about the movement of their temple flag. The first contends that it is the flag that is moving. The second insists that it is the *wind* that is moving. Into this heated dispute, Eno intervenes. "It is not the flag that moves," he informs them. "It is not the wind that moves. It is your *mind* that moves." The quarreling monks, so the story goes, are "awestruck" by Eno's observation.

In most commentaries on this story, Eno's pronouncement is understood to be a correction, if not a rebuke. Katsuki Sekida, an authority on Zen koans, interprets Eno's observation to mean, "Your mind is moving; don't let it move." This admonition, he adds, is "the warning of all Zen."

Perhaps so. But moving—generating thoughts—is what human minds do, twenty-four hours a day. Kosho Uchiyama, a twentieth-century Zen master, describes thoughts as the mind's "secretions," suggesting that the process of thought-creation is both natural and irrepressible. And broadly speaking, what Zen teachings discourage is not thinking *per se* but excessive thinking, which distracts us from present realities, and delusive thinking, which brings suffering upon ourselves and others. To counter both, the Zen tradition offers numerous teachings and practices.

Foremost among these is the practice of *zazen* (seated meditation). The classic posture of zazen, in which the two knees and the sitting bones form a triangle and the body a kind of pyramid, fosters stability of mind. To enhance that stability, Thich Nhat Hanh advises us to silently recite the verses, "Breathing in, I see myself as a mountain. / Breathing out, I feel solid." By so doing, we cultivate a feeling of solidity, emotional and physical.

In similar fashion, the practice of chanting reinforces a sense of stability. Zen practitioners chant from the lower abdomen. Sometimes accompanied by a wooden drum, the act of chanting unites the body, breath, and mind. In the Falling Leaf Sangha, our local Zen practice group, we precede our sittings with the chant "Atta Dipa," which is said to incorporate the Buddha's last words: *"Atta Dipa / Viharatha / Atta Sarana / Ananna Sarana // Dhamma Dipa / Dhamma Sarana / Ananna sarana"* ("*You are the Light / Rely on yourself / Do not rely on others / The Dharma is the light / Rely on the Dharma / Rely on nothing but the Dharma*"). In this context, "Dharma" may be interpreted as "the laws of reality," particularly those of impermanence and interconnectedness. By chanting "Atta Dipa," we declare our intention to rely on direct experience and remain grounded in things as they are.

Chanting and zazen are useful practices—"skillful means," Zen calls them—but it's important to remember their larger purpose, which is to situate ourselves in full awareness. As Jon Kabat-Zinn has observed, awareness is "infinitely available," and it is unperturbed by our changing states of mind:

> *Have you ever noticed that your awareness of pain is not in pain even when you are?... Have you ever noticed that your awareness of fear is not afraid even when you are terrified? Or that your awareness of your depression is not depressed; that your awareness of bad habits is not a slave to those habits?*

Extolling its power to transform pain, Kabat-Zinn likens awareness to a "basket for tenderly holding and intimately knowing our suffering in any and all circumstances." Our awareness is not angry when we are angry or sad when we are sad. It allows all things but is limited by none. In contrast to the forms that pass through it, awareness is formless and immovable.

"The enlightened mind," writes Sekida, "does not move." All too often, however, our not-yet-enlightened minds resemble that wind-blown flag, flapping this way and that. At such times, we can restore our equanimity by returning to the posture of meditation and resting in open awareness, which is never far to seek. On the contrary, it is readily accessible and reliably present, wherever we may be.

4 December 2014

O Great Mystery

*I*t's no great mystery, my friend used to say. He was a gifted mechanic and a natural handyman. How do you replace and properly gap the spark plugs on a '63 Ford pickup? It's no great mystery. Just read the manual. How do you fix a leaking toilet? Rewire an electrical outlet? No problem. And no great mystery either.

In practical terms, my friend may have been right, but in ultimate terms, he was wide of the mark. *O Magnum Mysterium* ("O Great Mystery"), a responsorial chant in the Roman Catholic Christmas Mass, celebrates the mystery of Jesus' birth in a lowly manger. In its reverence for the ineffable, as manifest in humble environs, that sacred text shares common ground with Zen teachings, which enjoin us to hearken, in a spirit of "not-knowing," to the hidden, unknowable, and indescribable dimension of ordinary life.

Stopping to buy a few fruits and vegetables at a roadside family farm, I linger to chat with the co-owner. She describes the process by which she and her husband make their own

Greek yogurt. I, in turn, report on a meal I concocted the night before: a medley of steamed kale, roasted bell peppers, and cashews served with quinoa. She says it sounds delicious. What could be more ordinary than our casual conversation, our brief exchange of words?

Yet what could be more mysterious, once you look into it—this capacity for thought, speech, and conversation, made possible by the human brain? Watching my eighteen-month-old granddaughter acquire words and concepts, I'm newly awed by the complexity and indeed the mystery of the process. According to the scientific findings reported by Alison Gopnik in her book *The Philosophical Baby*, there is far more thought, including thoughts of the past and future, going on in infants' and toddlers' brains than ever we imagined. And the same mystery surrounds the workings of our own, grown-up brains, which even the most advanced neuroscience has yet to fathom. Neuroscientists now understand single neurons and patterns of neurons fairly well, but how those neurons work together to produce an action remains unknown. How, asks Larry Abbott, a prominent neuroscientist, can one pattern of firing neurons "make you jump off the couch and run out the door, and others make you just sit there and do nothing?" That fundamental question has yet to be answered.

And as with the brain, so with the body. If you practice one or more of the so-called healing arts—Hatha Yoga, T'ai Chi, Qigong—you may have found that over time your bodily awareness has dramatically increased. You now notice minute changes in the form, strength, and flexibility of your limbs. Less happily, you also notice your most minor tensions, aches, and pains. But sensitivity is one thing and deep understanding quite another. For the latter, most of us must rely on health-care professionals to diagnose and treat our ills and maladies. And, as Dr. Jerome Groopman, in his book *How Doctors Think*, vividly illustrates, doctors themselves must rely on intuition and educated guesswork, as much as on their training, knowledge, and experience. "Medicine is an art, not a science," a local doctor informed me many years ago, as I lay in a hospital bed, recovering from a bleeding ulcer and wanting answers. More recently, when a dermatologist had examined a pesky skin disorder from which I'd been suffering, she offered what she called her "working hypothesis." Disconcerting though they may be, such remarks are also oddly reassuring. When all is said, the human body remains a mystery, and I'm relieved to hear experts humbly admitting as much.

Beyond the mysteries of mind and body, there is the profound mystery of death and its aftermath. Zen teachings call it the "Great Matter of Life and Death." In a famous Zen story, the eighteenth-century master Hakuin Ekaku encounters a samurai, who asks him what happens after death. "I don't know," Hakuin replies. "How can you not know?" the samurai retorts, "you're a Zen master." "Yes," replies Hakuin, "but not a dead one." Oft-repeated by contemporary teachers, that riposte epitomizes the general attitude of Western Zen to questions of death, rebirth, and the like. In contrast to other spiritual traditions, Buddhist included, Zen offers no maps, itineraries, or guidelines.

What Zen does offer is a practice through which we may cultivate an attitude of openness, awe, and appreciation toward the whole of life, including its mysterious, timeless dimension, which Shunryu Suzuki Roshi called "something which has no form and no color—something which exists before all forms and colors appear." In that connection, and in the spirit of the season, may I suggest listening afresh to the King's College Choir's 2009 rendition of Morten Lauridsen's *O Magnum Mysterium*, which interweaves dissonant, twentieth-century harmonies with an ancient text in a work of surpassing beauty.

18 December 2014

The Book of Janet

I have a friend by the name of Janet, who regularly consults what I call the Book of Janet, especially when she's feeling blue or vexed or insecure. If she makes some trivial error, like misplacing her car keys, the Book of Janet reminds her that she is not well-organized. If she enters a competition and receives a letter of rejection, the Book of Janet informs her that her work is not all that good. And if she's feeling less than beautiful on any given morning, the Book of Janet confirms her worst fears. On all three counts, the Book of Janet is wide of the mark. It is out of touch with the present reality. Unfortunately, that makes little difference to Janet, who swears by her Book as if it were her Bible.

Janet, I fear, is not alone. Most of us, I suspect, have a Book of Janet—or Josh, or Frank, or Amanda. And many of us carry our books with us throughout the day, making choices and judgments based on that fictive text. According to the Book of Benjamin, for example, I will not be happy if I don't begin the day with a pot of *sencha, fukamushi,* or *gyokuro* tea, fresh from Japan, brewed with pure water at precisely the right temperature and for exactly the right length of time. Reality may be otherwise, but that doesn't stop me from believing the Book of Benjamin and acting accordingly.

"In *my* book . . ." we sometimes say, as well we might. Our self-constructs and attendant guidelines help us navigate our days. But by clinging to those constructs or strictly complying with their constraints, we limit our possibilities for growth and full awareness. And according to Zen teachings, the very existence of such constructs is based on two fundamental misperceptions.

The first is that the bundle of attitudes, preferences, and habits known as Janet or Benjamin is a solid entity, possessed of an intrinsic essence and impervious to time and change. Where infants and toddlers are concerned, the error of this perception is readily apparent. Our children and grandchildren are changing before our very eyes. But in the world of grown-ups, an apparent sameness rather than an underlying impermanence may be a person's most salient feature, and a calcified habit may easily be mistaken for an enduring trait. Uncle Henry may be difficult, we say, but he is just being Uncle Henry. And if we turn the spotlight on ourselves, we may reach the same conclusion. How comforting it can be to define oneself as such-and-such ("I'm a purist"; "I'm an inveterate introvert") and attribute our choices, blunders, and triumphs to our inherent natures. But constructed self-definitions are one thing and true self-knowledge quite another. Vivid and compelling though they be, our labels may have little to do with the fluid aggregate to which they so tenaciously adhere.

The second misperception, no less beguiling than the first, is that the self exists in separation from the rest of the world. In our culture of individualism, we are conditioned to view the self in this way. We are seen—and may tend to see ourselves—as on our own. Yet even an irregularity as minor as a winter power outage should suffice to remind us that our autonomous selves co-exist in dynamic, interdependent relationships with nature and our fellow human beings. Should we look more deeply into the matter, we may also be reminded that what we call a self consists of "non-self" elements: the air we breathe, the water we drink, the food we consume. And should we choose to examine our emotional lives, we are likely to discover what Dr. Martin Luther King, Jr. called an "inescapable network of mutuality," in which our states of mind and indeed our spiritual condition are bound up with those of other living beings. As the Zen priest Norman Fischer eloquently puts it, "my suffering and your suffering are one suffering," and "that suffering is empty of any separation."

To remain continuously aware of the impermanence and interdependence of all life, as Zen teachings advise, is a daunting task. Prevalent forces in our society, including the denial of aging and death and the glorification of the youthful self, militate against it. But we can begin by discarding the notion of an unchanging, separate self embodied in a twice-told tale. With steadfast intention and diligent practice, it is possible to see through that illusion and recognize it as the life-denying obstacle it is. By so doing, we can open ourselves to selfless awareness and assume our rightful places in the unending stream of life.

5 February 2015

The Silence around the Words

Browsing the Internet one summer afternoon, I learned that Baltimore Orioles relish grape jelly. Cut an orange in half, my source instructed me, and place a dollop of grape jelly at the center of each half. Hang the halves from a branch, and you will soon have those beautiful birds in your own backyard.

Enticed by that prospect, I put grape jelly on our grocery list. And before long, I found myself in Aisle 10B at Wegman's Supermarket, searching for that elusive product.

"What are you looking for?" asked a petite, white-haired lady standing nearby, as she deposited a jar of Bonne Maman Apricot Preserves in her cart.

"Grape jelly," I replied. "Baltimore Orioles like it."

"They do?" she asked, giving me a wary, quizzical look, as though I had just said something very strange. "I never heard that. I used to live in Baltimore."

Realizing what had just occurred, I hastened to explain. "I mean the birds, not the baseball team."

"Oh," she sighed, visibly relieved. Meanwhile, I was imagining the Orioles in their dugout, passing around a jar of Welch's Grape Jelly. Perhaps that image had crossed her mind as well.

"What we've got here," remarks Paul Newman's Cool Hand Luke in the movie by that name, "is a failure to communicate." In the present case, what was lacking was a context, a verbal frame around the naked fact. But as Father Richard Rohr, a Franciscan priest and writer, has observed, what is often needed in our efforts to communicate and connect with other people is not more words but fewer. What is needed, he suggests, is the dimension of silence, which he figuratively describes as the "silence around the words." Absent that silence, much of our speech amounts to very little.

In Fr. Rohr's view, silence is more than an absence of sound. Silence, he asserts, possesses an "ontological identity," which is to say, it is a being in its own right. Most of our speech, for good or ill, is "ego-based." The ego uses words to get what it wants, employing argumentation, judgment, and analysis toward that end. Used in those ways, language is innately dualistic; it emphasizes preferences and differences. By contrast, silence "absorbs contradictions." It is a "wholeness of being" that "holds the contraries in a way that words cannot." When silence is absent, "words take over," producing a barrage of language whose purpose is to explain, sell, charm, persuade, punish, and the like. But when silence is present, "chaste, well-chosen words" can arise from the silence, words with silence around them. No longer based in a dualistic, "either/or consciousness," such words "open a portal to a deeper connection," both with the world of things and with other people.

Fr. Rohr's evocative description brings to mind a four-line poem by the Irish poet Michael Longley. Its subject is the poet's youngest grandchild:

> MAISIE AT DAWN
> *Wordless in dawnlight*
> *She talks to herself,*
> *Her speech-melody*
> *A waterlily budding.*

In these lines an attentive grandfather listens to the inarticulate sounds his granddaughter is making. Hearing them as a melody, he likens that melody to a waterlily on the verge of flowering. Just as Maisie's "speech-melody" has arisen out of the quietude of early morning, her first words are soon to emerge as the flower of language. Longley's haiku-like poem is at once a loving study of a child and a contemplation of the mystery of silence, sound, and language. By leaving much unsaid, Longley's spare words evoke the silence around them.

Zen has been called the study of silence. The practice is more than that, of course. But by sitting still, even for the space of twenty minutes, we can allow our minds to settle and our inner chatter to diminish. Resting in open awareness, we can sense the eternal silence beneath the onrushing images, memories, and other mental phenomena. By making that silence the object of contemplation, we can witness the arising of thoughts and their emotional subtexts from the depths of silence and the ocean of consciousness. And should we then choose to speak, our words are far more likely to connect us with nature, ourselves, and other people, whether our subject is the appetites of Baltimore Orioles or the murmurings of an awakening child.

5 March 2015

Healing is Possible

In the Parable of the Burning House, a revered text in the Zen tradition, a grand but dilapidated mansion catches fire. At the time, the wealthy owner is standing outside the gate, but inside the mansion, his three sons are playing with their toys, oblivious of the encroaching conflagration. Rushing into the house, their father implores them to get out, but they ignore his admonitions. To entice them, he promises to give them jeweled, ox-drawn carts if they will leave. By these "expedient means" he achieves his purpose, and his sons escape "the burning house of the threefold world." Soon afterward, their father presents them with magnificent carriages adorned with gold, silver, and pearls and drawn by stalwart, pure-white oxen. Released from the burning house and their former attachments, his sons enjoy safety and freedom.

I was reminded of this parable while reading Allan Lokos's new book *Through the Flames*, which recounts Lokos's experience of a horrific plane crash and his near-miraculous survival and recovery. In December 2012, Lokos and his wife, Susanna Weiss, were enjoying a ten-day holiday in Myanmar. On Christmas Day, they boarded a short flight from Mandalay to Inle Lake. As their low-flying plane approached its destination, it struck electrical wires, burst into flames, and crashed in a rice field. Susanna jumped to safety from a side exit, but Allan, who was just behind her, caught his foot on something and suffered burns to a third of his body before he could escape. In the anguished days that followed, doctors in Myanmar, Bangkok, and Singapore informed Susanna that her husband, whose burns were massive and bone-deep, could not possibly survive, let alone recover.

Yet recover he did, thanks in part to his meditative practice. Allan Lokos is the founder and guiding teacher of the Community Meditation Center in New York City. In telling his story, he gratefully acknowledges the roles of his supportive wife, his generous friends, and his compassionate surgeons in his recovery. He recalls the encouraging words of Dr. Tan Bien Keem of Singapore, who told Lokos that when he cut into his patient's body he felt "an energy—a life-force—that was too powerful to die at that time." But most of all, Lokos attributes his survival, his relatively swift recovery, and his present equanimity to the Buddhist teachings he had absorbed and practiced for many years prior to his trauma.

Prominent among those teachings is the principle of "dependent origination," which holds that every event is the natural consequence of causes and conditions. "This is, because that is," the teachings tell us. "This ceases to be, because that ceases to be." Applying this principle to his own experience, Lokos describes it in this way:

> *A pilot brought a plane down short of a runway. The plane, flying low, cut through electrical wires and sparked a fire that engulfed the plane. The plane crashed. I tried to jump from the plane but my foot got caught on something and I was seriously burned before I could free myself. My mind/body immediately went into survival mode and I did survive.*

Void of hyperbole, Lokos's prose plainly states what happened. As he acknowledges, and as his book vividly demonstrates, his experience entailed "a great deal of physical, mental, and emotional pain," and at times during his recovery, the insight of dependent origination was "not enough to fill the emotional emptiness." But by focusing, as best he could, on the actual causes and conditions of the crash, rather than speculate on what might have been, he freed himself from the "infinite number of story lines, projections, and perceptions we can attach to such an event." By eschewing "regrets, accusations, or blame," and by refraining from asking unanswerable questions ("Why me?"), he allowed "the road to recovery to be unencumbered." Primarily for that reason, he believes, he has healed more smoothly and rapidly than anyone had expected.

Standard interpretations of the Parable of the Burning House view the burning mansion as *samsara*—the realm of suffering, driven by greed, anger, and a fundamental ignorance of reality. The rescuing father is the Buddha, who guides resistant humanity toward wisdom and liberation. And the jeweled carriages represent the "vehicle," the teachings and practices that convey the practitioner from suffering to happiness. In Allan Lokos's case, those teachings and practices were already in place, and they allowed him "to stay grounded not only in the chaos and urgency of the crash but also in the dark days that followed." Lokos believes that with patience and determination, "complete healing is possible, even when a cure is not." And though his narrative is graphically detailed and often unsettling, it is also deeply inspiring. "Doctors said I would not live," he recalls. "They meant well, but they were wrong. I am healing. You can too."

2 April 2015

Ethical Attentiveness

Reading a brochure from the Laz-y-Boy company the other day, I came upon the claim that Laz-y-Boy, Inc. is "being mindful" with respect to the environment. I was heartened to find that reassurance, but I couldn't help wondering whether the company was voicing an authentic concern or merely striking a fashionable attitude.

Over the past two decades, the practice of mindfulness has assumed a prominent place in American life. In the vernacular of our times, mindfulness has gone mainstream. American corporations, particularly those situated in Silicon Valley, have embraced the practice, chiefly as a means of reducing stress and increasing productivity. So have the military academies, the health-care system, the prison system, and, more gradually, public schools and higher education. Yet, as the practice has gained in acceptance, it has sometimes lost sight of its origins in Buddhist meditation, and a central component has often been left behind.

That component is the ethical dimension, especially as it pertains to the practitioner's emotional life. In his book *Living with Awareness*, the Buddhist monk and scholar Sangharakshita (formerly Dennis Lingwood) reminds us of this important dimension of the practice:

> *To be human is to inhabit a realm in which ethical responsibility is not only possible but requisite. Thus, mindfulness must be understood to be more than simple concentration: we need to be as clear as we can about the nature of what we are doing and why. A murderer intent upon his victim is certainly concentrating, but that kind of single-mindedness is very different from the ethical attentiveness that characterizes a state of true mindfulness.*

As these remarks suggest, "ethical attentiveness" begins with awareness of what we are doing at any given moment and the impact of our actions on the rest of the world. If, for example, we are playing loud music or talking into a cell phone in a public space, true mindfulness will remind us that we are contributing to noise pollution and diminishing the peace and well-being of other people. Merely by being present for our actions, we can recognize when we are causing harm and when we are not.

Beyond this basic social awareness, the practice of mindfulness can also awaken us to the ethical content of our feelings, thoughts, and states of mind. *The Four Foundations of Mindfulness (Satipatthana Sutra)*, a core text for the practice, enjoins us to identify our present, transitory feelings (that is, sensations) as "pleasant," "unpleasant," or "neutral." We are also directed to examine the "roots and fruits" of our feelings, distinguishing between "worldly," ego-based feelings such as craving and aversion, and "unworldly" feelings such as compassion and sympathetic joy, which are grounded in selfless awareness.

By watching our feelings in this way, even as they are arising, maturing, and disappearing, we can learn to observe how pleasant, unpleasant, and neutral sensations engender our emotions and mental states, which last much longer than feelings and often result in speech and action, whether harmful or beneficial. We can note how a spark of anger can become the flames of rage, or a tinge of melancholy spiral into depression. With practice, we can also learn to distinguish between so-called "unwholesome" mental states, such as craving, hatred, and delusion, and "wholesome" states like concentration, loving-kindness, and equanimity. By bringing awareness to our unwholesome states of mind, we decrease their potential to harm ourselves and others. Fully aware of our lust or anger, we are less likely to translate those mental states into speech or action. Conversely, by recognizing and actively contemplating our wholesome states of mind, we can strengthen their force in our daily lives. In Buddhist meditative practice, specific contemplations are devoted expressly to that purpose.

The English word mindfulness is a translation of the Pali word *sati*, which derives from a root meaning "to remember." In part, the practice of mindfulness consists of remembering to be present for the present moment—to "keep our appointment with life," as Thich Nhat Hanh would put it. But in its deeper, original context, the practice also consists of remembering to recognize, identify, and monitor our changing feelings, emotions, and states of mind and their influence on the conduct of our lives. "One thing you need to remember and understand," observes the Burmese master Sayadaw U Tejaniya, "is that you cannot leave the mind alone. It needs to be watched constantly. If you do not look after your garden it will overgrow with weeds. If you do not watch your mind, defilements will grow and multiply. The mind does not belong to you, but you are responsible for it."

Continuously responsible, I might add, even when you are surfing the Internet—or relaxing in your Laz-y-Boy recliner.

14 May 2015

Living with Dignity

*I*n contemporary public discourse, it has become common to speak of "dying with dignity," especially in discussions of assisted suicide. By contrast, it is rare to find a reference to *living* with dignity, except when it pertains to the elderly or disabled or infirm. Yet what could be more important to our well-being, one might ask, than living with dignity, whether one is healthy or sick, youthful or advanced in years?

Like other spiritual traditions, Zen Buddhism regards dignity as an innate and defining quality of human beings. It is the birthright of every living person. In his essay "Giving Dignity to Life," the American Buddhist monk Bhikkhu Bodhi puts it this way:

> *For Buddhism the innate dignity of human beings . . . stems . . . from the exalted place of human beings in the broad expanse of sentient existence. . . . What makes human life so special is that human beings have a capacity for moral choice that is not shared by other types of beings.*

As Bhikkhu Bodhi goes on to say, human dignity is both an inborn potential in human beings and a quality to be cultivated through disciplined effort. Through daily meditative practice and the exercise of our unique capacity for moral choice, we can "actualize our potential for dignity."

In Buddhist meditation, as in other Eastern traditions, mind and body are seen as inextricable. And in practice, the cultivation of dignity can begin with moment-by-moment awareness of the body, including its positions, movements, and anatomical parts. Significantly, the four basic positions of the body—sitting, standing, walking, and lying down—are known in Buddhist teachings as the Four Dignities. And in systematic practice, each of the Four Dignities becomes an object of mindful awareness. When Jon Kabat-Zinn, founder of Mindfulness-Based Stress Reduction, advises practitioners to "sit in a way that embodies dignity," he is echoing the Buddhist origins of his secular program. Similar admonitions accompany the practice of walking meditation, as when Thich Nhat Hanh urges us to "walk like a free person," and Jack Kornfield advises us to walk slowly and with regal dignity, as if we were royalty out for stroll.

Beyond this attention to posture and movement, the quality of dignity can be cultivated through silent contemplation. We can become what we contemplate. Of the many objects of contemplation available to the practitioner, two are of particular importance.

The first of these is the contemplation of impermanence, not as an abstract concept but as an immediate reality. It is one thing to affirm the proposition that "everything changes." It's quite another to accept the reality of unrelenting change, especially when a loved one is involved, and the change is catastrophic. Yet, if we can truly accept the darker side of impermanence, our acceptance can lend dignity to our lives. Sakyong Mipham, a teacher in the Tibetan Buddhist tradition, explains:

> No matter how we want to cling to our loved ones, by nature every relationship is a meeting and a parting. This doesn't mean we have less love. It means we have less fixation, less pain. It means we have more freedom and appreciation, because we can relax into the ebb and flow of life. Understanding the meaning of impermanence makes us less desperate people. It gives us dignity.

As Mipham's observation suggests, there is a direct connection between awareness of impermanence and the realization of personal dignity. The one engenders the other.

And just as a deep acceptance of impermanence can foster dignity of heart and mind, so can the cultivation of the mental state known as *upeksha*, or equanimity. The most exalted of the "Four Immeasurable Minds," equanimity might be defined, in simplest terms, as a quality of balanced awareness when encountering life's vicissitudes. Not to be confused with indifference, the mind of equanimity is engaged, warmly and compassionately, with whatever occurs, but it is not overwhelmed. For Westerners who might wish to contemplate an image of equanimity, I would suggest Robert Frost's sonnet "The Silken Tent," in which Frost likens his wife to a silken tent "loosely bound / By countless ties of love and thought" and supported by a "central cedar pole." "Strictly held" by none of her obligations, she "gently sways at ease." Frost originally titled the poem "In Praise of Her Poise."

With stories of warring states and terrorist atrocities dominating the news cycle, it often seems that dignity is in short supply. Indeed, the concept of human dignity is most often invoked in the context of human rights—and gross violations thereof. But in our everyday lives, as in our interactions with others, dignity is not only a possibility but a living presence, however neglected or obscured. Like a secluded garden in a noisy, violent city, it has only to be tended.

18 June 2015

Steady Attention

"If you are truly present for an orange," Zen master Thich Nhat Hanh once remarked, "the orange will be present for you."

I was reminded of that remark when viewing the recent exhibition of sixty black-and-white photographs by the photojournalist Caroline Littell (1939-2015) at Alfred University's Herrick Memorial Library. Entitled "Camera without Borders: The World of Caroline Littell," this wide-ranging exhibition was curated by her husband, the travel writer Alan Littell, and their son Harry Littell, Associate Professor of Photography at Tompkins Cortland Community College.

As variegated as it is accomplished, Caroline Littell's work spans several decades and the multiple continents she visited during her lifetime. Her beautifully rendered photographs, nearly all of them predating the digital era, were taken in countries as diverse in character and terrain as Burma, Botswana, Thailand, Colombia, Scotland, Turkey, Canada, and the United States. Many portray indigenous inhabitants, singly or in groups. Others depict landscapes, public squares, churches, monuments, and wild animals in their natural habitats. Diverse as they are in subject, however, the photos evince two consistent qualities, which together convey a strong sense of presence, whether the subject is a rhino in Tanzania or two young men astride their motorbikes on a street corner in Bangkok.

On the one hand, the photos achieve, time and again, an effect of spontaneous immediacy, akin to that of a snapshot. Unstaged and uncontrived, they capture a fleeting moment just as it was. In one stark but subtle photo, taken in Metsovo, Greece, two elderly women in black headscarves and long black dresses climb a sidewalk against the backdrop of a white stone wall. One follows the other, but although they are in step, each appears engrossed in her own thoughts. Here as elsewhere, the photo creates the sense of the moment unfolding, unhindered by the medium or the will of the photojournalist to control what she is encountering.

At the same time, Littell's composition is artfully balanced. And even in her most kinetic images, a sense of the transitory moment is countered by a feeling of sustained attention. That is particularly true of her panoramic renditions of unpopulated landscapes, which range from the Scottish Highlands to the Sussex Downs to a snowy field in Alfred, New York. Viewing these tranquil images, their quietude enhanced by their monochromatic medium, I am left with an impression of steady, unhurried observation.

Of the many photos that join a sense of the world in continuous motion with that of poised, relaxed attention, one of the most memorable is a picture of fishermen in a boat on Inle Lake in Myanmar, formerly known as Burma. I first viewed this photograph in the late 1980s, when it appeared in print in conjunction with a travel article by Alan Littell. The image impressed me at the time, and viewing it again, nearly thirty years later, I find it no less compelling.

Against a faintly discernible horizon obscured by a dense mist, three Burmese fishermen are at work on narrow boats resembling dugout canoes. Two are attending to large conical fishing nets. Closest to the camera stands an oarsman, his left foot planted on the stern and his right leg curled around a tall wooden oar. He appears to be rowing—or about to row—the long boat with his leg, as is the custom on Inle Lake, where the heavy vegetation on the water makes a seated rowing position impractical. The oarsman's dark reflection shimmers in the slightly rippling water. Although the boat appears to be in motion, and the men are busy with their labors, this symmetrical, unruffled image is imbued with a mood of contemplative calm, reminiscent of Asian minimalist painting. Though firmly embedded in time, it has the timeless character of a haiku.

"What you look hard at," wrote the poet Gerard Manley Hopkins in his journal in 1871, "seems to look hard at you." As her choice of subjects indicates—she was an explorer and documentarian, not an investigative journalist—and as her posthumous exhibition amply demonstrated, Caroline Littell's approach to her subjects was more intuitive than hard, more empathic than interrogatory. But in her unending curiosity, her openness to experience, and especially her capacity to wait for the instant when the character of a person, place, or thing might disclose itself, she allowed her subjects to speak for themselves. Patiently present for the world's ephemeral forms, she made them vividly present for her viewers.

23 July 2015

True Intimacy

*I*n its most common usage, the word intimacy hardly suggests a spiritual context. Enter the word in your browser, and you are likely to turn up references to the bedroom, the boudoir, and Britney Spears' line of designer lingerie. Yet the root of *intimate*, from which *intimacy* derives, is the Latin *intimus*, which means "inmost." And a desire for true intimacy—for connection with one's inmost nature—is fundamental to many spiritual traditions, Zen Buddhism included. "Intimacy," writes the Zen teacher Jakusho Kwong, "is at the heart of all of Zen."

In formal Zen practice, the cultivation of intimacy begins with mindfulness of breathing. Toward that end, basic instructions for Zen meditation direct the practitioner to count breaths, "follow the breath," or employ meditative verses in conjunction with the respiratory cycle. "Breathing in, I know I am breathing in," reads one such verse, "Breathing out, I know I am breathing out." These methods are useful, especially for beginners. They focus attention and calm the body-mind.

Whether they foster intimacy is another matter. To begin with, "the breath" is an abstract concept, and like other abstract concepts, it promotes the illusory notion that what it signifies is a solid thing—or, more exactly, a string of solid things: a series of discrete, countable breaths, rather than the continuous, fluctuating process it actually is. No less important, formulations for observing the breath can easily become the primary focus of concentration. Preoccupied with numbers or words, we may find ourselves intently counting those numbers or listening to the words, as if they and not our breathing were the objects of attention. Hard at work, we may inadvertently distance ourselves from our immediate experience.

Should that occur, the practitioner has other options. In my own practice I have found it helpful to concentrate on the *sensations* of breathing, wherever they might be felt. Breathing is an autonomic, complex, and mysterious activity. By adopting an attitude of humility, and by resolving merely to feel our breathing rather than measure or label it, we can allow the process to continue just as it is. By relinquishing any effort to lengthen or otherwise manipulate our respiration, we permit ourselves to enter its mystery, as intimately as possible.

And as with breathing, so with the body. Teachers of meditation sometimes advise their students to do a "body scan" before settling into a period of sitting. Beginning with the lower body and proceeding upward, or, conversely, scanning from the top down, the practitioner directs awareness to general regions or specific parts of the body: "Aware of my shoulders, I breathe in. / Bringing kind attention to my shoulders, I breathe out." The effect is to relax tense muscles, quiet the nerves, and ease the body as a whole.

Body scans can reveal hidden tensions and imbalances. They can prepare us for extended sittings. But like conscious breathing, systematic scans can sometimes interfere with our direct experience. At a retreat some twenty years ago, Thich Nhat Hanh urged us to listen to our bodies and recognize whatever might be "calling" us, bringing mindfulness to that place. Over the years, I have found that simple stratagem effective. More intuitive than methodical, it promotes a closeness with one's physical being. By listening receptively rather than asserting control, we permit reclusive knots to disclose and release themselves. And we also become aware, in real time, of the moment-by-moment changes occurring within us.

Those changes are mental and emotional as well as physical. And, just as we can become intimate with our physical being, we can also become intimate with the flux of our thoughts, feelings, and states of mind, even as they are occurring. Pausing periodically throughout the day to monitor that flux, we can readily perceive the changeability of our mental states. We may notice that we are feeling anxious and angry in the early morning—and equable an hour later. Through the disciplined practices of sitting and walking meditation, we heighten and refine that broad recognition, becoming ever more aware of the subtlest tonal changes.

In so doing, we may also become aware of the energy behind those changes: what the Zen teacher Shohaku Okumura has called "the universal life force." When we open our awareness to the impermanence of all conditioned things, as manifest in our breathing, our bodies, and our inner lives, we open ourselves to that "universal life force," allowing it, in Okumura's phrase, "to practice *through* us for the benefit of all beings." Although it defies description, that force can be felt in the wind and sun and rain as well as in ourselves. It can heard in the din of traffic. Opening ourselves to its presence, we cultivate intimacy with life itself.

20 August 2015

The Music of Constancy

"As everyone knows," declares Ishmael, the narrator of Herman Melville's novel *Moby-Dick* (1851), "meditation and water are wedded forever."

Melville's schoolmaster-turned-sailor makes this remark in the opening pages of *Moby-Dick*, as he reflects on the lure of water, especially to those of a contemplative disposition, who are naturally drawn to ponds, lakes, rivers, and the sea. Ishmael is not a meditative practitioner in any formal sense, and as Daniel Herman, a Melville scholar and Zen practitioner, notes, "Melville almost certainly never in his life heard the word 'Zen'." Yet Ishmael's remark is relevant to the discipline of Zen meditation, insofar as that remark calls attention to two salient elements of the practice. By its nature, water visibly embodies the quality of impermanence, one of the primary objects of Zen contemplation. At the same time, water also embodies the quality of constancy, which Zen teachings urge us to contemplate. "How can I enter Zen?" a student asked a master. "Can you hear the murmuring of the mountain stream?" the master replied. "Enter there."

The law of impermanence (*annica*) is one of the cornerstones of classical Zen teachings. "All composite things," the *Diamond Sutra* enjoins us to remember, are "like a dewdrop . . . a bubble in a stream." If we wish to become intimate with impermanence, we have only to look inward, observing our thoughts and feelings as they arise, abide for a while, and disappear. And should we choose to look outward, we can turn our attention to the phenomenon of water in its manifold forms and changes. Those changes may be dramatic, as when waves crash into rocks or white water tumbles over a waterfall. They may also be gradual and subtle, as when dewdrops evaporate or a dense fog lifts or the bubbles in a stream dissolve. But whether the changes are obvious or covert, water affords the contemplative mind an apt and endlessly eventful object. In its presence, we can readily observe what the poet Seamus Heaney, speaking of the river Bann, called "the steady go of the world."

Yet, even as we are doing so, we are also contemplating constancy. Rivers, to be sure, are notoriously unpredictable. And with our growing awareness of climate change, oceans are no longer the emblems of constancy they once appeared to be. Those realities notwithstanding, however, bodies of water in general and lakes and pools in particular afford us rest and solace. They calm our unquiet minds. And if poets and artists of a meditative temperament—John Constable, William Wordsworth, Heaney, Elizabeth Bishop, to name a few—have often gravitated toward water and incorporated images of lakes, ponds, and pools in their works, it is in part because the imagery of still water reflects the composure of the contemplative mind. And for those of a more intuitive nature, the abiding presence of water, however dynamic, may also evoke the ineffable, immutable dimension of human experience.

So it was with the British contemplative poet Charles Tomlinson, who died last month at the age of eighty-eight. In his poem "Movements," he records his sense of continuity amidst fluid change:

> *"Written on water," one might say*
> *Of each day's flux and lapse,*
> > *But to speak of water is to entertain the image*
> *Of its seamless momentum once again,*
> > *To hear in its wash and grip on stone*
> *A music of constancy behind*
> > *The wide promiscuity of acquaintanceship,*
> *Links of water chiming on one another,*
> > *Water-ways permeating the rock of time.*

In the passage from which these lines are taken, Tomlinson is recalling his nightly visits to a deep, silent pool, a "visible church, where everything / Seemed to be at pause, yet nothing was." In the presence of those tranquil waters, he sensed the constancy of an "unending present, traveling through / All that we were to see and know."

Zen teachings admonish us to be mindful of "each day's flux and lapse" and the impermanent nature of all conditioned things. We suffer, Thich Nhat Hanh reminds us, not because things are impermanent but because we expect them to be permanent when they are not. Yet, according to the *Dhammapada*, a foundational text for Zen practice, mindfulness is also "the way to the changeless." By giving wholehearted attention to the unending present, we become acutely aware of the world of forms and their unending changes. But if we are fully attentive, we may also intuit the timeless, formless dimension of our experience, from which forms arise and to which they return. Listening to links of water chiming on one another, we hear, as it were, the music of impermanence. But can we also incline our minds, as Buddhist teachings advise, toward the changeless? Can we hear, however faint its strains, the music of constancy?

10 September 2015

Soft Eyes

One afternoon a few summers ago, I decided to practice the guitar on our backyard deck. It was a sunny day, the temperature in the mid-seventies. At the time, I was revisiting the *Prelude* from J.S. Bach's *Prelude, Fugue, and Allegro* (BWV 998), a piece I had played for years and knew by heart. Normally, I practice indoors, my eyes fixed on the score. If I've memorized the piece, I tend to stare at the fingerboard, as classical guitarists are prone to do. That afternoon, however, I looked out at our spacious and secluded backyard, where the natural world was vividly in motion. Blue jays were foraging in the grass. Leaves quivered in a light wind. High in a tall pine, a dark bird flew in, perched for a moment, and flew out. As I played the first few bars of the *Prelude*—a lyrical but technically challenging piece—my eyes came to rest on our Curly Willow tree in the middle distance. At the same time, I remained keenly aware of all the peripheral movement. And as I proceeded into the *Prelude*, I gradually realized that my playing had become more fluent and relaxed. To my surprise, it had also become more accurate, expressive, and rhythmically precise.

That experience was new to me, but it was hardly my invention. Without knowledge or systematic training, I had stumbled upon a technique known to equestrians, martial artists, and other highly skilled performers as "soft eyes." "Do you know what you need at a crime scene?" asks Detective Bunk Moreland in *The Wire*. "Rubber gloves?" ventures Detective Kima Greggs. "Soft eyes," Moreland replies. "You got soft eyes, you see the whole thing." In essence an integration of peripheral and foveal (central, line-of-sight) vision, the technique of soft eyes is used in fields as diverse as tracking, performance driving, interior decorating, teaching, yoga, and Akido. The personal and social benefits of this technique can be significant, if not transformative. It can permit us at any moment to see "the whole thing." Yet in obvious ways, the practice of soft eyes runs counter to the prevalence of "hard eyes"—the type of vision we habitually employ when chopping a carrot or threading a needle or working at a computer. To learn to look with soft eyes may require conscious effort.

If you would like to explore this technique, I would recommend that you choose an outdoor setting, preferably a wide-open area. Select an object in the middle distance, and focus your powers of concentration solely on that object, as though you were trying to grasp it with your eyes. When you have done this for a minute or more, relax your eyes, allowing your vision to soften. Letting your attention rest on the object, imagine that you are inviting and receiving it, just as it is, into your consciousness. At the same time, allow your perspective to widen, noticing how other objects and movements, sensed or actually seen, emerge in your peripheral vision. Open your hearing as well as your sight, and note the changes occurring in your body, your state of mind, and your general awareness.

Those changes may be pronounced, especially if you cultivate the practice over time. In *The Breathing Book*, the yoga teacher Donna Farhi directs us to observe how the practice of soft eyes opens and broadens the diaphragm, relaxing and deepening our breathing. And in *Centered Riding*, the equestrian teacher Sally Swift provides a detailed discussion of the soft-eyes technique, which she defines as "a method of becoming distinctly aware of what is going on around you, beneath you, inside of you." Practicing with soft eyes, young riders learn to relax themselves and their horses and to remain aware of everyone else in the arena. Professional riders also employ the technique to competitive advantage. As Swift notes, the celebrated American equestrian Denny Emerson developed the skill of switching back and forth between hard and soft eyes, as needed, during competitive events.

The term soft eyes is rarely heard in Zen circles, and the concept of softness may seem at odds with the austerities of Zen discipline. As it happens, however, classical instructions for *zazen* (seated meditation) advise us to keep our eyes half-open and our gaze trained on a point three feet in front of us. Easing and slightly blurring our visual perception, we then expand our peripheral vision as widely as possible, as we become quietly aware of whatever is occurring within and around us. According to an old Zen story, one accomplished Rinzai master, practicing in this way, could sense a fly landing behind him—or two, if they happened to mating. That story may be apocryphal, but it well illustrates the principle and the virtue of soft eyes.

1 October 2015

The Study of Silence

Zen has been called the study of silence. "We need silence," writes Zen master Thich Nhat Hanh, "just as much as we need air, just as much as plants need light." But how, exactly, are we to study silence? By what means can we cultivate its nourishing presence?

Just be quiet, one is tempted to suggest. *Just be still.* But in a world rife with noise and distraction, that choice may no longer seem plausible—or even very desirable. In her book *Reclaiming Conversation*, the sociologist Sherry Turkle reports that many of the people she has interviewed, particularly young people, have an aversion to silence, finding it merely boring. They would rather go online. And as Thich Nhat Hanh observes in his book *Silence*, many of us are afraid to sit quietly, doing nothing. By keeping ourselves ever-busy and ever-connected, we avoid such negative feelings as loneliness, restlessness, and sadness, which can become all too present when we are silent and alone. If we wish to study and cultivate silence, it would seem, we have first to overcome our resistance, whether it be grounded in aversion or fear.

Having accomplished that first step, we may also need to revise our concept of silence, which is often viewed as an absence of sound. It is difficult to contemplate an absence, much less an absence as abstract as silence. Father Richard Rohr, a Franciscan priest who has written extensively on this subject, urges us to grant silence an "ontological identity," which is to say, to view it as having a real and even palpable presence and a being of its own. Rather than conceive of silence in terms of what it is not, we can concentrate on what it *is*, whether the silence we are contemplating is external or internal: the silence immanent in our surroundings or the silence deep within ourselves.

As our daily experience will readily attest, external silence can be hard to come by. Libraries and doctors' waiting rooms are no longer silent places, and the once-quiet lounges of American airports are now polluted by voices on cell phones and the endless drone of CNN. And that is to say nothing of the ambient commercial music in malls, restaurants, shops, and public spaces. The physicist George Prochnik, who studies acoustic phenomena, believes that as a culture we are currently experiencing an "epidemic of excessive acoustical stimulation," much of it injurious to our health and equanimity. "Noise," he laments, "is defiantly on the rise." Conditioned if not exhausted by the din in the public arena, we may need to remind ourselves that in our private domains, silence is still an option. Laptops, TV's, mobile devices, and even noisy appliances can be turned off. Idle chat can be held in abeyance. And should we wish to experience sustained periods of silence, we can seek out quiet places. We can take a walk in the woods, or attend a Quaker meeting, or commit to a silent retreat.

Silencing our inner noise is another matter. Once we have found or created a silent space, how are we to silence our interior monologues, which can be as loud or louder than our surroundings? Methods vary, but in my experience one of the most effective ways to quell our inner noise is to shift our orientation from our hyperactive minds to our oft-neglected bodies. This can be done while engaging in physical activity—walking, swimming, yoga, T'ai Chi—but it is most readily accomplished by stopping whatever we are doing and sitting still, our spines upright, our eyes softly focused on a point three feet in front of us, our bodies aligned and relaxed. Bringing awareness first to our breathing and subsequently to whatever physical tensions we may be experiencing, we allow our mysterious bodies to find their own balance. Under such conditions, gaps may open in our unending stream of thought. Quite often, our inner chatter will diminish or disappear of its own accord.

If we persist in this practice, lengthening our sittings to thirty minutes or more, we can learn to "protract the gap": to dwell without fear or aversion in the intervals between our successive thoughts. Recognizing the empty, impermanent nature of our thoughts, feelings, and states of mind, we can release them whenever they are ready to go. By so doing, we not only pacify our minds and relinquish our discursive and often judgmental thinking. We also open ourselves to what the Japanese philosopher Shizuteru Ueda has called the "space of the unfathomable stillness, or absolute silence." Always present but only rarely acknowledged, that deeper silence nourishes and sustains us. And when, as we must, we reenter the realm of thought and speech, it endows our words with depth and meaning.

22 October 2015

A Mind that Alights Nowhere

As a boy growing up in eastern Iowa, I savored the word *dwell*, which I heard on many a Sunday morning. *I will dwell in the house of the Lord forever*, I intoned with the rest of the congregation, not quite understanding the context but reassured by the general idea. The word was pleasant to pronounce. It made a pleasing sound.

Only later did I learn that *dwell* bears a negative connotation. "Don't dwell on it," I was advised, in the aftermath of some abrasive encounter. "She didn't mean to hurt your feelings." Used in that fashion, *dwell* meant to brood, to worry, to concentrate unhealthily on some slight or insult or perceived injustice. Nowadays, for good or ill, many people use the verb *obsess* to describe the same habit of mind. "Don't obsess about it," we might advise a person who can't stop talking about a personal dilemma, or can't let go of a painful experience, as though that person had a choice, or our well-intentioned counsel might be helpful.

According to Zen teachings, we *do* have a choice, but if we wish to exercise that choice, we have first to distinguish between obsessive dwelling and sustained contemplation. Zen master Thich Nhat Hanh encourages meditative practitioners to stop and "look deeply" into the present moment. By dwelling, in this constructive way, on immediate realities, we can lessen the suffering that our hurried, egocentric, and often erroneous perceptions inflict on ourselves and others. Intuiting that the rude young woman who has just offended you may herself be a victim of abuse or neglect, or that the man whose arrogance you find so annoying might be chronically insecure—such insights, the fruits of "looking deeply," can awaken our innate wisdom and compassion. By the same token, dwelling on a sacred text or a meditative slogan can illuminate one's present condition.

Obsessive rumination is quite another thing. The practice of contemplation is associated with such wholesome states of mind as openness, empathy, mindfulness, and concentration. By contrast, rumination is most often driven by unwholesome states, among them fear, anger, envy, and greed. In the Theravadan Buddhist tradition, practitioners learn to recognize the mental states of craving, aversion, and ignorance—the "three poisons" of classic Buddhist teachings—by observing the effects of those states on their minds and bodies. Craving creates a sense of grasping and contraction, aversion a sensation of pushing away. Ignorance engenders a feeling of running in circles, endlessly and uselessly. If you are susceptible, as I am, to obsessive thinking, you may have experienced all of these sensations, as you grasped for a solution to a difficult problem, pushed away suggested remedies, and felt your mind revolving in familiar grooves of thought.

So far as I know, there is no simple cure for compulsive thinking. It is less an ailment than a temperamental condition. Help may be found, however, in a practice from the Vipassana ("Insight") meditative tradition. Known as "noting" or "labeling," this practice consists of naming whatever process is occurring in our minds at any given moment. Becoming aware that we are thinking in abstractions, rather than being present for our immediate surroundings, we note: *thinking, thinking.* Realizing that we are thinking, relentlessly and needlessly, about the future, we might label our activity *what-if, what-if.* Observing ourselves in the act of remembering—or reliving—an experience, we back away far enough to label that process: *remembering, remembering.* As we become more practiced in this method, we can learn to sense the feeling beneath or around the obsessive thought: the emotional subtext that is causing us to worry or plan or lose ourselves in the past. Beneath incessant planning, for example, we might detect unrecognized fear or ungratified desire or a deep-seated need for control.

The practice of noting can generate liberating insights. It can reacquaint us with our own minds. Its most immediate benefit, however, is a furlough from the prison of obsessive thought. This can happen within a matter of minutes. And over time, Zen teachings promise, the practice can transform the most anxious cast of mind into what the *Diamond Sutra* calls "a mind that alights nowhere": that no longer clings to its objects of attention. Released from habitual patterns of thought and feeling, we can elect to dwell (in the wholesome sense) on an object of interest, giving that object our wholehearted regard. Conversely, we can merely note what is occurring, within and around us, whether it be a pang of grief or a memory from childhood or the bark of a neighbor's dog. Moving at will between these modes of knowing, we can enlist the one that best serves our highest intentions, our immediate circumstances, and our present state of mind. And that way freedom lies.

12 November 2015

Give it All Away

The practice of Zen contemplation, Zen teachings tell us, is the "action of non-action," grounded in silent awareness. At the same time, the "non-action" of Zen is best described in active verbs. In her essay "What is Zen?" Shinge Roko Sherry Chayat Roshi offers this description:

> *What is Zen? Stop now. Stop trying to get an intellectual lock on something that is vast and boundless, far more than the rational mind can grasp. Just breathe in with full awareness. Taste the breath. Appreciate it fully. Now breathe out, slowly, with equal appreciation. Give it all away; hold onto nothing. Breathe in with gratitude; breathe out with love. Receiving and offering—this is what we are doing each time we inhale and exhale. To do so with conscious awareness, on a regular basis, is the transformative practice we call Zen.*

It would be difficult to find a more lucid or concrete description of Zen practice. Follow Shinge Roshi's instructions, and you will not go wrong. Yet, for all its clarity, this description is at one point ambiguous. "Hold onto nothing," Shinge Roshi advises. "Give it all away." But what is the antecedent, a grammarian might inquire, of the pronoun "it"? What, besides our breath, are we giving away?

To begin with, if we are to undertake the practice of Zen in any serious way, we must be willing to examine our ingrained habits of mind, most centrally the habit of intellectualizing our experience. Almost from the cradle we are taught and conditioned to "try to get an intellectual lock" on whatever we encounter: to define, compare, categorize, and analyze our immediate experience. To this process we bring our memory of past experiences, our language (or languages), and our powers of discrimination. For better or worse, we may also bring our fixed ideas, preferences, and expectations, our notions of how things ought to be. All of this is necessary for our survival. By such means we keep our bearings and navigate a complex social reality. Unfortunately, our familiar concepts and our conditioned habits of mind, however useful or productive, can prevent us from being present for what is occurring in the here and now. If we are to meet the present moment on its own terms, and if we aspire to open ourselves to what is "vast and boundless" in human experience, we have first to relinquish our calcified views, our comfortable assumptions, and our habitual patterns of conceptual thought.

Among the views that bind us, none is more prevalent or conducive to suffering than the notion of a separate self. In our culture of individualism, that notion is often taken as axiomatic and reinforced at every turn. We drive, often alone, in separate vehicles; we guard and maintain our private fiefdoms; we celebrate the successful, independent man or woman. In reality, however, we are at once independent and interdependent, autonomous and enmeshed in the dynamic web of life. In Zen teachings, the interdependent self is sometimes likened to a wave on the ocean or a whirlpool in a stream. An impermanent thing-in-itself, it depends upon other selves, which is to say, on other people for its continuing existence. And just as the self is interconnected with other human beings, it is also interdependent with the natural world, of which it is an inextricable part. "Wherever you are," wrote Shunryu Suzuki Roshi, "you are one with the clouds and one with the sun and the stars that you see. You are still one with everything." By renouncing the notion of a separate self, we open ourselves to the realization of this abiding oneness. No longer confined to our separate precincts, we manifest the boundless depth of our true nature.

By cultivating awareness of the impermanence and interdependence—what Zen calls the "emptiness"—of all conditioned things, we also cultivate our innate capacity for wisdom and compassion. "Realization of emptiness," wrote the Tibetan sage Milarepa (1040-1123), "engenders compassion." When we practice *zazen* (seated meditation), regularly and diligently, bringing our hearts as well as our minds to the practice, we are not only giving away our cherished likes and dislikes, our proclivity to judge and discriminate, and our dualistic notion of "self and other"—itself a source of untold suffering. We are also, in the phrase of Zoketsu Norman Fischer Roshi, "training in compassion," moment by moment, and carrying that training into our daily round. Breathing in, we endeavor to appreciate our precious human lives.

In a spirit of gratitude, we gather our energies and our sense of a stable self. Breathing out, we "give it all away," offering to suffering humanity, near and far, whatever insight we may possess, whatever equanimity we might embody, and whatever help we might provide.

3 December 2015

The Gift of Non-Fear

Last week two Army helicopters flew over the village of Alfred, New York. Their thunder, my wife confided, unnerved her as never before.

In the wake of the mass shootings in Paris, Colorado Springs, and San Bernadino, fear has become a focus of national attention. In his address to the nation on December 6, President Obama sought to reassure us. "Freedom," he asserted, "is more powerful than fear." Perhaps it is in the long run, but for the time being, how can we best address the growing presence of fear in our daily lives? And how can the practice of meditation help us in that effort?

Generally speaking, Zen teachings admonish us to sit erect, practice conscious breathing, and cultivate awareness of whatever is occurring, within and around us. Can we "turn toward [our] fears," asks the Zen teacher Zenkei Blanche Hartman, "and be with them with kindness and gentleness?" If we can, that shift of attitude alone can do much to calm the fearful mind. But if we are in need of a more systematic approach, we can also explore a method known as R.A.I.N., developed by the mindfulness teacher Michele McDonald. The acronym R.A.I.N. stands for Recognition, Acceptance, Investigation, and Non-Identification. This proven method may be brought to bear upon any state of mind, in this instance fear.

Recognition

The first step in this practice is the simple acknowledgement that fear is present. When many of us experience fear, especially unfamiliar fear, we may deny it, or turn away from it, or busy ourselves with other matters. Fear is sometimes viewed as a weakness; it can be difficult to admit, even to ourselves, that we are afraid. For some people, the act of naming ("fear is present"; "fear is happening") can be useful. So can the recitation of *gathas*, or meditative verses: "Breathing in, I know that fear is in me; / Breathing out, I recognize that fear is in me." Whatever our method, the essential practice is to recognize that fear is present.

Acceptance

Having acknowledged the presence of fear, can we then accept it? Can we allow it space, and even welcome it into our lives?

Truly to "be with" our fears, we have first to acknowledge and be with our conditioned resistance. This resistance may take the form of repression, self-judgment ("What's wrong with me?"), or other, more subtle forms of defense and rejection. And we may also need to remind ourselves that acceptance is not mere passivity or craven resignation. Acceptance is an active process, in which we have agency. By actively saying "yes" to our fears, we are not capitulating or giving in to our weaker side. Rather, we are treating our fears with kindness and respect, allowing their energies to arise, abide, and disperse of their own accord.

Investigation

"What is this?" asks a classic Zen koan. By asking that question repeatedly, followed by "I don't know," we come to realize the impermanent nature of phenomena and the true nature of mind.

That same question can be asked of our fears. Fear induces contraction. How does that contraction feel in our bodies? In our hearts and minds? What are its roots in our conditioning? In our felt experience?

In conducting this inquiry, we are not engaging in amateur psychoanalysis. Nor are we imposing concepts or theoretical constructs on our immediate experience. Quite the opposite: we are contemplating an aspect of our experience with the aid of intuition and the intention of gaining insight into the nature and origin of our fears. With insight comes relief from suffering—and eventual liberation.

Non-identification

Just as we can come to understand the roots of our fears in our conditioning, we can also explore and understand those aspects of our fears that only appear to be personal. Fears may arise from causes and conditions that have little or nothing to do with us as individuals. They pass through us like currents in a river or clouds in the sky. By identifying with our fears ("I'm a fearful person"; "I'm such a wimp"), we mistake impersonal realities for personal qualities. Conversely, by relinquishing the habit of identification and by understanding our fears as selfless, impermanent phenomena, we release ourselves from self-confinement and self-inflicted suffering. Resting in open awareness, which isn't afraid when we're afraid, we observe our transient fears arise and subside, but we are no longer in their thrall.

A gift

The practice of R.A.I.N. is no quick fix. It requires us to be present for our forgetfulness, our resistance, our indifference to our own emotions, and especially our penchant for taking things personally. It also demands patience and persistence. But if we elect to pursue this practice, it can alleviate our fears and gradually transform them. In this holiday season, the practice can be a gift to others and ourselves.

17 December 2015

A Permanent Beginning

Last month the holiday season brought three small grandchildren to our home. Jack is six, Isla three, and Allegra two. Three may well be a crowd, but apart from an upset or two, this trio of tots played harmoniously together, and their brief presence brightened our lives.

A few days after the children and their parents had departed, I retired to my study to read a book I had bought just before the holidays: *The Essential Brendan Kennelly*, a richly varied selection of the Irish poet's work, published on the occasion of his 75th birthday. I had left the book on a low table next to my reading chair. When I opened it, I found to my surprise a waxy red scribble on the title page. Someone had left me a souvenir.

Although I am not one to condone the defacing of books, I was amused by this discovery, and I suspect that Brendan Kennelly would be as well. One of Kennelly's best-known poems, "Poem from a Three Year Old," speaks in the voice of a child. Its exuberant verses dramatize the spirit of play, the incessant questioning, and the moments of wonder intrinsic to childhood. "The first moment of wonder," Kennelly has remarked, "is an amazing moment, as if for the first time something is happening. And that is the moment on which poetry depends." There is a "strange thing" in us, Kennelly asserts, that is destroyed by familiarity and experience. But through the successive acts of attention that constitute an authentic poem, the familiar can again become strange and the sense of wonder restored. "And I think that's what poetry is about—a kind of permanent beginning."

Kennelly's view of poetry informs his poem "Begin," written in the poet's fifties while he was recovering from heart surgery. Set in central Dublin, this poem portrays the narrator awakening on a spring day to the sounds of birdsong and morning traffic. Observing a "pageant of queuing girls," he celebrates the "exaltation of springtime" and the mood of hope the season affords. At the same time, he acknowledges that "every beginning is a promise / born in light and dying in dark." And as he notes the bridges on Dublin's Grand Canal, which "[link] the past and future," he is reminded of deceased friends who remain alive in memory. In the remainder of the poem, the tone continues to darken, and literal observation gives way to general reflection:

> *Begin to the loneliness that cannot end*
> *since it perhaps is what makes us begin,*
> *begin to wonder at unknown faces*
> *at crying birds in the sudden rain*
> *at branches stark in the willing sunlight*
> *at seagulls foraging for bread*
> *at couples sharing a sunny secret*
> *alone together while making good.*

Though we live in a world that dreams of ending
that always seems about to give in
something that will not acknowledge conclusion
insists that we forever begin.

In these lines, as in the poem generally, images of sunlight, warmth, and intimacy coexist with images of isolation, distress, barrenness, and hunger. The sense of wonder that Kennelly associates with childhood is balanced against a seasoned adult's experience of death and loss. And the sense of beginning, which the poem joyously extols, is tempered by a mature awareness of inevitable endings.

According to Zen teachings, each moment of our experience is unprecedented and unrepeatable. We would do well to accord it our full attention. But, as Kennelly's poem exquisitely demonstrates, the light-filled wonder we may feel at any moment is of a piece with our darkest thoughts. On this sunny January morning, as I look out on our peaceful, snow-covered yard, I am struck once again by the beauty of the natural world. At the same time, I am mindful of the sufferings of family and friends. One is battling an aggressive cancer; another is mourning with dignity and grace his wife's recent passing; and a third, who will soon turn ninety-three, is living alone with his cat and his memories of service in World War Two. With each new breath, they—and I—begin again.

14 January 2016

What It Means to be Present

One bright morning several weeks ago, I received a friendly e-mail message from Amazon. "Benjamin W. Howard," it read, "Based on your recent activity, we thought you might be interested in this:" Below these words, a handsome new book was displayed: *Firewood and Ashes: New and Selected Poems,* by Ben Howard."

To be fair to Amazon, I was indeed interested in the product described, and my interest was indubitably based on my recent activity. And, all things considered, I was heartened to see Amazon actively marketing my book and targeting a plausible customer. More power to them, I might have said, and may their project flourish.

At the same time, Amazon's little slip-up highlighted something fundamental and unnerving about life in the digital era. Like other denizens of the twenty-first century, I am aware of the ways by which mega-conglomerates monitor our purchasing histories and manipulate our predilections. Nonetheless, had the book being promoted not been my own, I might have dozily surmised that someone at Amazon was looking out for me, as old-fashioned booksellers used to do, and that the message I had just received embodied an actual human presence.

In reality, the presence on my laptop screen was virtual in every sense of the word. It was a fabrication generated, I assume, by an impersonal algorithm. More disturbingly, the deceptive resemblance to a real human presence was almost certainly no accident. In his book *The Four-Dimensional Human*, an engrossing reflection on "ways of being in the digital world," Laurence Scott observes that "[c]onsumerism has traditionally thrived in the real world from our having fixed, demographically analyzable identities. For this reason its agents are understandably keen to minimize the differences between our material and digital lives, to erode the boundaries between the real and the virtual." Amazon and its like not only monitor the preferences of our demographic selves; they also "promote a conflation of reality and virtuality." As we have become ever more immersed in digital culture, both the term and the concept of "presence" have grown ever more problematic. "The big bold future," Scott predicts, "will demand an evolution in how we think about *what it means to be present*, how we manifest bodily and virtually in the world."

Dr. Tara Brach, a clinical psychologist and founder of the Insight Meditation Community in Washington, D.C., has thought long and hard about what it means to present. And in her book *True Refuge*, she offers this explanation of the term: "Presence is not some exotic state that we need to search for or manufacture. In the simplest terms, *it is the felt sense of wakefulness, openness, and tenderness that arises when we are fully here and now with our experience*. You've surely tasted presence, even if you didn't call it that. Perhaps you've felt it lying awake in bed and listening to crickets on a summer night. . . . You might have arrived in full presence as you witnessed someone dying or being born." By *wakefulness* Dr. Brach means "the intelligence that recognizes the changing flow of moment-by-moment experience," including our thoughts and bodily sensations. By *openness* she means the non-judgmental "space of awareness" that allows our emotional lives to be just as they are, without interference or evaluation. And by *tenderness* she means the capacity to respond to our immediate experience with warmth, awe, and compassion. Together these qualities constitute what Dr. Brach calls "natural presence," which she likens to a "sunlit sky." Presence of this kind cannot be willfully activated, but it can be accessed and cultivated, primarily through the practice of meditation. By regularly practicing sitting and walking meditation, or merely by pausing for short periods during our daily round, we allow ourselves to "come back to presence" and to live our lives in mindful awareness.

Natural presence may seem categorically different from the virtual presences we daily encounter on our computer screens. Whatever else it might have projected, the message I received from Amazon did not embody wakefulness, openness, or warmth. Yet, in the digital age, the distinction between virtual and actual presence is not always so simple or clear. Laurence Scott notes that "if our bodies have traditionally provided the basic outline of our presence in the world, then we can't enter a networked environment . . . without rethinking the scope and limits of embodiment." As an example, he tells the story of a "smitten grandpa" in Pennsylvania who uses state-of-the-art technology to keep in touch with his granddaughter. "I have *face time*," Grandpa reports, "every week with my sixteen-month-old granddaughter while she's eating her dinner, and when she says goodbye she hugs the iPad." A smitten grandpa myself, I have had the very same experience, though our own, two-and-a-half- year-old granddaughter goes so far as to kiss the screen. Virtual and natural presence coalesce, in ways I appreciate but haven't begun to fathom.

4 February 2016

The Inevitable Attenuations

In an interview many years ago, a journalist asked the Irish poet Seamus Heaney (1939-2013) for his thoughts on aging. At the time, Heaney must have been in his late fifties or early sixties. With his usual precision of language, leavened by a wryly ironic smile, Heaney remarked that growing older had brought "the inevitable attenuations." He did not elaborate, but anyone of a certain age could readily fill in the blanks. And more important than the words or the missing details was the attitude behind them, an attitude at once rare and profoundly liberating.

Like forty million other men and women over the age of fifty, I belong to the AARP, formerly known as the American Association of Retired Persons. As a privilege of membership I receive two bimonthly publications: the *AARP Magazine*, which is printed on glossy paper and vaguely resembles *People* magazine; and the *AARP Bulletin*, which is printed on newsprint and resembles a tabloid. The *Magazine* endeavors to entertain, educate, and inspire me, while perhaps selling an Acorn Stairlift or a life-insurance policy along the way. By contrast, the *Bulletin* aspires to keep me informed and alert me to financial and health-related hazards threatening older people. Together these complementary organs of our consumer culture purport to enhance my so-called golden years and help me feel more secure. All too often, however, their effect is quite the opposite.

The *AARP Magazine* celebrates celebrities. The cover of the current (December 2015/January 2016) issue features a 70-year-old Diane Keaton wearing a stylish hat, a sporty black jacket, and an oversized pinstriped shirt, tucked into her loose-fitting jeans. Thin as a stalk of asparagus, she is smiling broadly. Should that image entice us, we can open the magazine to Meg Grant's feature article, where we learn that Diane is "always, literally, on the move . . . In addition to acting, she writes. She takes photographs. She sings!" In a sidebar, Diane also gossips about "her leading men," among them Robert de Niro, Warren Beatty, and Al Pacino. Not lacking in financial resources, Diane likes to indulge her "passion for serial nesting," and so far she has "renovated a least a dozen houses." Her compulsion to keep creating new homes is, in Keaton's words, "a fantasy of [creating] a new you."

Perhaps there are well-heeled readers, themselves intent on creating new you's, who find such stories inspiring. But for those of us who are neither rich nor famous nor in a position to experiment with serial nesting, the emotional impact is likely to be otherwise. Not only do the annals of celebrity culture invite comparison and its attendant envy. They can also stir the latent fear that our own lives have never been and will never be the equal, in glamour, wealth, mobility, and fulfillment, to those of the stars. One is almost relieved to learn that Burt Reynolds, at the age of 79, "has no woman in his life." Perhaps he should give the footloose Diane a call.

If the *AARP Magazine* sets our unconscious fears in motion, the *AARP Bulletin* shifts them into overdrive. The lead story in the current *Bulletin* concerns "New Scams to Avoid." Prominent among them are phone scams offering technical support for non-existent computer viruses. But we should also watch out for "chip card" and IRS imposters eager to gain access to our financial records and our life savings. No doubt such perils are real, and AARP is doing a service to potential victims of fraud and corporate manipulation, but the high concentration of such warnings in a small space, cheek by jowl with ads for hearing aids, Safe Step Walk-in Tubs, "Risk-free Cellphones," and Medical Alert monitors, tends to unnerve rather than reassure the patient reader. And, not incidentally, it also conditions us to keep reading the *AARP Bulletin*, lest we miss reports on the latest menacing news.

How refreshing, by contrast, are Seamus Heaney's well-chosen words, which neither fuel our illusions nor scare us out of our wits. "Inevitable" derives from the root *evire*, which means "shun" or "avoid," and the closest synonym to "inevitable" is "unavoidable." "Attenuate" derives from the Latin *attenuare*, which means "to make thin." As electronics technicians know, an attenuator is a device that diminishes the amplitude of a sound without distorting its waveform. To describe the changes that come with advancing age as "inevitable attenuations" is to tell, however abstractly and obliquely, the unvarnished truth. And, as with the old Zen saying "The elbow does not bend outward," the effect of Heaney's phrase is strangely tonic. Bringing us home to the reality of our lives, Heaney's words free us from denial and liberate us from delusion. And paradoxically, by returning us to full awareness, they open us to our own boundless nature, in a way that a hundred tales of happy celebrities could never do.

18 February 2016

A Time to Let Go

On this snowy winter evening I've been listening to Benjamin Britten's *Nocturnal After John Dowland* (1963), a twenty-minute piece for solo guitar composed for the English lutenist and guitarist Julian Bream (b. 1933). By turns dreamy and martial, restless and serene, this masterpiece of the modern guitar repertoire can be heard on Bream's 1967 album *20th Century Guitar*, one of forty CD's in my newly-acquired *Julian Bream: The Complete RCA Album Collection* (2013). Released in conjunction with Bream's eightieth birthday, this handsome boxed set is both a treasure trove of music for classical guitar and a tribute to a great musician's lifetime achievement. And for this listener, the collection also evokes an enduring memory.

Deep in the winter of 1970, Julian Bream gave a concert at Alfred University. I was then a young assistant professor of English and a part-time lecturer in music. To my delight, I was entrusted with picking up Mr. Bream at the Rochester airport on the day before his concert, taking him to dinner, and getting him settled in the university's guest apartment. Going well beyond the call of duty, I subsequently enticed Julian to join me for a few pints at the university's (then) on-campus pub, where we stayed on until the closing hour. The topics of our rambling conversation included aspects of the guitar and guitar technique; his student days at London's Royal Academy of Music, where he studied piano and cello; the jazz guitarist Django Reinhardt, whom he avidly admired; George Harrison, whom he'd met at a party the week before; his recent audience with Queen Elizabeth II, on the occasion of his receiving the OBE (Order of the British Empire) for his "services to music"; and the winter landscape of Western New York, which reminded him of the rolling farmland of Wiltshire, where he owned thirty acres and lived in a Georgian farmhouse. Toward the end of our conversation, he remarked that what he'd learned at the Royal Academy had been of limited use to him later on. Music itself had been his teacher. What mattered most, he felt, was having a passion for whatever one was doing.

Julian Bream's passion for music, translated into artistic conviction, can be felt throughout his recordings, whether he is playing a Renaissance air, a Bach fugue, or a commissioned work by a contemporary composer. Musical passion is everywhere present in Bream's rendition of the *Nocturnal*, which features bold, non-tonal intervals, sharply contrasting textures, and breakneck runs brilliantly executed. "A modern work," Bream noted in 1974, "may have strange qualities which may be rather new for many listeners. So you really have got to muster up as much conviction in your performance as possible." Muster it he did, time and again, and the force of that conviction, supported by impeccable phrasing and prodigious technique, distinguishes his performances from those of most of his contemporaries.

All the more poignant, then, was Bream's decision, in 2011, to relinquish the making of music. In 1984, Bream had crashed his car into a railway bridge, smashing the bones in his right elbow. Fortunately, he soon recovered, relearning the guitar and continuing to perform until his retirement in 2002. Nine years later, however, as he was walking the fields around his home with his black retriever, Django, a neighbor's dog knocked him down, breaking both his hips and injuring his left hand. After the first accident, Bream recalls, he had "refused to let go." But after the second, he elected to do just that. "How much are you playing these days?" the *Guardian*'s Stuart Jeffries asked him in 2013. "Not at all," he replied, adding that there was "nothing sad about not playing anymore." Instead he was reading, listening to music, and taking walks with Django. Was he renouncing the world, asked Jeffries, "as Buddhists recommend?" "In a controlled way," Bream replied. He had "cut away" the "excess stuff in [his] life," moving from his country home to a bungalow in a nearby village. He'd had a "lovely life," but now it was "time to let go."

In an oddly parallel fashion, the trajectory of Julian Bream's career resembles that of the *Nocturnal*, which consists of eight variations on the theme of John Dowland's lute song "Come, Heavy Sleep" (1597). Reversing the usual order, Britten presents the variations first and the theme at the end. The variations are harmonically complex, their technical demands severe. "The *Nocturnal* was very nearly beyond me," Bream later admitted, recalling the ten days he spent at Robert Graves's house in Majorca, practicing the piece in a shepherd's hut on the poet's property. But in the closing section of the *Nocturnal*, the composer returns to his source, and the high drama of Britten's variations is resolved in the simple beauty of Dowland's song. "Slow and quiet (*molto tranquillo*)," the score prescribes. And though the song is tinged with melancholy, the mood is one of arrival and repose.

3 March 2016

One Particular Action

"Why do we like being Irish?" asks the Irish poet Louis MacNeice (1907-1963) in his poem *Autumn Journal* (1939). In subsequent lines, he answers his own question:

> Partly because
> > It gives us a hold on the sentimental English
>
> As members of a world that never was,
> > Baptized with fairy water;
>
> And partly because Ireland is small enough
> > To be still thought of with a family feeling,
>
> And because the waves are rough
> > That split her from a more commercial culture;
>
> And because one feels that here at least one can
> > Do local work which is not at the world's mercy
>
> And that on this tiny stage with luck a man
> > Might see the end of one particular action.

Because Ireland is a relatively small country, and because in MacNeice's time families tended to stay put for as long as economic conditions allowed, Irish people could reasonably hope to see the "end"—the consequences as well as the completion—of any particular action.

In Zen teachings the relationship of actions and their consequences is known as *karma*. The word karma means "action," and it is often paired with *vipaka*, which means "result." "The simplest formulation of karma," writes the Zen teacher Zoketsu Norman Fischer, "is actually quite straightforward: if this, then that. In other words, actions have consequences." Those actions include acts of the body, speech, and mind, and all have a moral dimension. The so-called law of karma, as Fischer sees it, is "a kind of moral physics." Actions have "moral power." By following Zen precepts, and by ever increasing our awareness of our bodies, speech, and thoughts, we endeavor to "do good action" and "avoid bad action." In this way we generate what Zen calls "wholesome" rather than "unwholesome" karma.

In popular usage karma is often regarded as an individual matter. People speak of "my karma" as though it were theirs alone. But, as MacNeice well understood, and the poet W.B. Yeats before him, entire cultures also have their karma, whether wholesome or unwholesome or some mixture of the two. "Great hatred, little room," wrote Yeats in 1931, eight years after the end of the Irish Civil War. And MacNeice, likening the abstract, feminine idea of "Ireland" to a transitory "patch of sun on the rainy hill," complains that "we love her for ever and hate our neighbor / And each one in his will / Binds his heirs to continuance of hatred."

Yet change is possible. Karmic patterns can be interrupted. And for the Zen practitioner the primary agent of change is a full and continuous awareness of what is occurring within and around us. In popular culture karma is often equated with preordained fate: we are wedded to our karma. But according to classical Buddhist teachings, just the opposite is the case. In any given moment we are not only experiencing the results of our past actions but also creating new karma. Results are becoming causes. Whether our present actions will help to break ingrained, destructive habits of thought and feeling, or merely deepen their grooves in our psyches, will depend on whether we are living at that moment in full awareness. Having just been subjected to a subtle or not-so-subtle slight, or having heard an opinion we don't agree with, can we fully recognize, in real time, what is occurring? Can we align our response with our best intentions, rather than react from a place of fear or anger? According to the oft-cited findings of the neurosurgeon Benjamin Libet, we have only a quarter-second in which to choose how to respond, but choose we often can. Among other possibilities, we can elect to listen rather than speak. And if we persist in the practice, our capacity to respond wisely rather than react reflexively can be strengthened.

In the late 1990s Norman Fischer conducted "sitting-talking-listening" retreats in various venues, among them a peace conference in Belfast, Northern Ireland. Participants in the Belfast retreat, he reported, "remarked that it was no wonder that the Protestants and Catholics of Northern Ireland could not get along. How could they even begin to make peace if they literally couldn't hear what the other side was saying?" Conversely, participants also discovered, in

Fischer's words, "how wonderful it was to listen, and to be able to speak when someone else was actually listening." To be sure, the significance of this one particular action, occurring against an historical backdrop of grief and grievance, should not be exaggerated. But by such means and through such actions, what Zen calls "karmic seeds" are sewn, and over time they can generate new and constructive results, whether in Northern Ireland or here at home, in our own, deeply divided polity.

17 March 2016

My Unexpected Teacher

When the student is ready, the teacher will appear. So goes the Zen proverb, and for many it may be true. In my case, however, I was neither ready nor expectant. And my first guide on the path of meditation was an unlikely candidate for the position.

Allen Ginsberg visited Alfred University in October 1978. It was a relatively tranquil time, especially when contrasted with our present era. A few weeks earlier, the Camp David Accords had been signed under the watchful eye of President Jimmy Carter. In Western New York the fall colors were at their peak.

In my personal life, a kindred stability prevailed, however illusory it would prove to be. I was then a young associate professor of English, newly tenured and recently returned from a sabbatical in Cambridge, England. A budding Anglophile, I sported a Harris tweed jacket and smoked a meerschaum pipe (though I did not inhale). In matters personal as well as professional, I cultivated a decorous reserve.

Perhaps Allen Ginsberg sensed as much when I met him at the Elmira airport. He arrived in the company of Peter Orlovsky, his ruggedly handsome companion. Ginsberg was then in his early fifties, and next to the athletic Orlovsky he looked rather sedentary, though comfortable in his casual attire, a purple handbag over his shoulder. He wore thick glasses and a salt-and-pepper beard.

"Why did you invite me?" he asked, as we walked to the luggage carousel.

The question caught me off-guard. "Well, because . . . I respect your work," I replied.

That was hardly the warmest response I might have mustered, but at least it was honest. As a literary specialist, I appreciated the importance of Ginsberg's poem "Howl" in reshaping the landscape of American poetry. And as the director of the university's Visiting Writers series, I had indeed invited Ginsberg to our community. But at the time I gravitated toward the traditional rather than the avant-garde in contemporary verse, and though I admired the lapidary poems of Gary Snyder, I had little time for the Beat writers or their theory of spontaneous composition ("First thought, best thought"). And had I been asked, I would have expressed more tolerance than enthusiasm for Ginsberg's celebrated persona—that of the disruptive, unruly political radical.

Yet, over the next three days, my narrow perceptions would widen, my prejudices dissolve. During his three-day residency, Ginsberg gave an exuberant reading (where he recited the entirety of "Howl"), delivered a scholarly lecture on modernist poetics, engaged in lively conversations with students, and joined my first wife and me for dinner at our wood-heated farmhouse. A generous, sweet-tempered man, he treated everyone with courtesy and respect, and he seemed more interested in looking and listening than in expounding his opinions. "What is that bush called?" he asked me, noticing the red-leaved sumac along Elm Valley Road.

In one of our conversations, the subject of meditation came up, and when a few of us expressed an interest, Ginsberg offered to teach us how to sit. We agreed to meet the following morning in the Octagon (c. 1850), a village landmark, where a colleague had set up house.

In accordance with beliefs current at the time of its construction, the Octagon contained no square corners where the Devil could hide. Spiders and dust balls, yes, but devils, no. In that improbable setting, we novices received basic instruction in sitting meditation. *Keep your eyes half-open. Let your breath go out to the objects in the room. On your in-breath, take a vacation.* We sat for perhaps a half hour, after which our teacher gave an impromptu talk on the Buddhist doctrine of emptiness. *Picture a bare branch against the sky*, he told us. See it in its *suchness*, void of any meanings we might attach to it.

Ginsberg left the next day, and I never saw him again, though he later sent me the typescripts of two poems written during his visit. Nonetheless, that visit had made an indelible impression. For all my innocence of Buddhist meditation, I had felt the groundedness of Ginsberg's posture, the solidity of his practice, and the uncommon clarity of his thought. In the months to come I would have need of those qualities, as long-standing marital issues came to a head and precipitated an emotional crisis. And over the next two decades, a journey that began in the Octagon would lead to annual retreats with the Vietnamese Zen master Thich Nhat

Hanh, residencies at meditative centers in England, Ireland, and North America, and, in November 2002, to the taking of vows and precepts at Dai Bosatsu Zendo, confirming my commitment to Zen practice. For guidance along the way, I have many people to thank, but no one more than my first, unexpected teacher.

31 March 2016

Every Day is a Good Day

Among the cryptic sayings associated with the Zen tradition, none is better known than that of Ummon Bun'en (862-949), who famously declared that "every day is a good day." Yeah, right, the weary, seasoned mind replies. Tell that to the commuter caught in gridlock or the stressed-out parent nursing a sick child. Superficially construed, Ummon's remark sounds both naive and culpably aloof.

Yet, if examined in the light of Zen teachings, this adage is neither foolish nor untrue. The key component of Case 6 of the *Blue Cliff Record*, a classic collection of Zen koans, Ummon's pronouncement is a fiction that points to an underlying reality, a construct that discloses a deeper truth. If we wish to probe that truth, we can consult the host of commentaries Case 6 has accrued, beginning with that of Hakuin Ekaku (1686-1768), compiler of Zen koans, who called this particular koan "cold," meaning austere and challenging to contemplate. But if we wish to explore Ummon's saying in a warmer light, we can begin by reflecting on how we know, or think we know, the things of this world, and how we determine whether a given day is good or bad.

Picture two-and-a-half-year-old Carter sitting on the living-room rug, accompanied by his great-aunt Robin, a sketch pad before them. Carter chooses a marker from the box of markers, and with a vigorous tug he pulls off the cap. It's a skill he's recently acquired, and it gives him satisfaction. Employing the same force with which he sends his toy cars racing across our hardwood floors and crashing into the baseboards (no harm done), Carter presses the tip of his chosen marker on the blank page of the sketch pad, inscribing a robust line.

"What a nice line!" exclaims Aunt Robin. "Fuchsia!"

"Fuchsia," replies Carter, adding another line, "is a kind of pink."

It has taken only a few seconds, this process of cognition. First came raw sensation: the feel of the felt tip pressing the paper, the sudden arrival of vivid color on the page. Next, with a little help from his great-aunt, came the name of the color. And last came the definition, category, and subcategory, which he had heard and absorbed the previous day. Carter is now in possession of a new grain of knowledge—knowledge that will help him navigate the world and perhaps to compete in a complex culture.

In years to come, Carter may discover more about the color *fuchsia*. From his Uncle Ben he may learn that fuchsia refers to a kind of flower, which grows wild in the West of Ireland. When his great-uncle lived on the Beara Peninsula, he saw wild fuchsia cascading down a cliff to the sea. From his classmates Carter may learn that pink, the genus of which fuchsia is a species, is considered a girl's color. If he harbors a fondness for that color, he would do well to keep it to himself.

Meanwhile, the beauty and mystery of the color and his own excitement in first encountering it will have diminished or vanished altogether. Knowledge and social conditioning will have subsumed his sense of wonder.

But let us now imagine that Carter, advanced in his middle years, decides to take up the practice of Zen, having read one of his late great-uncle's books on the subject. He will begin by learning to sit still, in a relaxed, upright posture, following his breath. In a few months' time, he may develop enough stability to look directly and deeply into his present experience. And after a few years of practice, during which he will have become ever more intimate with his inner life, he may discover that there is a gap of awareness between his raw sensations and his ensuing perceptions, and that with diligent practice he can learn to prolong that gap and to rest in the openness of awareness. Within that sky-like space, his most anxious thoughts will be seen for what they are: empty, impermanent forms, which arise, endure for a while, then disappear. Likewise his layers of social conditioning, which include the dualistic constructions of "self" and "other," "beautiful" and "ugly," "good" and "bad," may begin to fall away, and he may find that the forms and colors of this world, including the color fuchsia, will have become fresh once again, as though he were encountering them for the first time. In this exalted state, which Zen calls *positive samadhi*, he will find his mind clear and his sense of wonder restored. And should he come to abide in samadhi, day in and day out, every day will indeed become a good day, irrespective of the season, the weather, or whatever sorrows life might throw his way.

21 April 2016

NOTES

The Greene Street Feeder

3 **"With people and things . . ."**: This admonition appears in a well-known poem by Layman P'ang (740–808), a celebrated practictioner ("There's nothing different in my everyday affairs . . ."). See William Scott Wilson, *The One Taste of Truth* (Shambhala, 2012), 78.

The Straightforward Mind

10 **In his commentary on *jikishin kore dojo***: William Scott Wilson, 50. Wilson translates *jikishin* as the "straightforward mind." In *The Vimalakirti Sutra* (Columbia University Press, 1997), Burton Watson translates the Chinese term *chih-hsin* (*jikishin*) as "upright mind," but in a footnote he writes that *chih-hsin* "may also be translated 'straightforward mind' or 'direct mind.'"

"As human beings . . .": Roshi Bernie Glassman, "Bear Witness to All of Life" (*Shambhala Sun*, May 2013), 57.

Wild Surmise

14 **As the Venerable Henepola Gunaratana explains**: Venerable Henepola Gunaratana, *Mindfulness in Plain English* (Wisdom, 1991), 152.

14 **And with practice**: Nyanaponika Thera, *The Heart of Buddhist Meditation* (Weiser, 1988), 35.

Awful but Cheerful

16 **"Don't say, 'It is beautiful . . .'"**: E. L. Mayo, "Old Knifedge," *Collected Poems* (New Letters, 1981), 82.

18 **"If you really want to see something . . ."**: Howard Nemerov, "On Metaphor," *The Howard Nemerov Reader* (University of Missouri, 1991), 223.

True Realism

19 **In a recent column**: Paul Krugman, "The Chutzpah Caucus," *New York Times*, May 5, 2013.

This Precious Human Birth

23 **As the Zen teacher Norman Fischer explains**: Norman Fischer, *Training in Compassion: Zen Teachings on the Practice of Lojong* (Shambhala, 2012), xvi-xvii.

Open and Shut

26 **In this column**: Frank Bruni, "Who Needs Reporters?" *New York Times*, June 1, 2013.

27 **For as Elizabeth Mattis-Namgyel**: Elizabeth Mattis-Namgyel, "The Power of an Open Question," *The Best Buddhist Writing 2011*, ed. Melvin McLeod (Shambhala, 2011), 139.

The Weirs of Age

29 **A river flows past**: Shohaku Okumura, *Living by Vow* (Wisdom, 2012), 158-159.

31 **As Thich Nhat Hanh observes**: Thich Nhat Hanh, "Can Nothing Become Something?" *Thich Nhat Hanh Dharma Talks*, http://tnhaudio.org/tag/flame/.

"The weirs of age": Edwin Arlington Robinson, "Eros Turannos."

We can also learn: Melissa Myozen Blacker, "No is Not the Opposite of Anything," *The Book of Mu* (Wisdom, 2011), ed. James Ishmael Ford and Melissa Myozen Blacker, Kindle edition, 2243.

Clear Seeing

33 **As Chodron notes**: Pema Chodron, "5 Reasons to Meditate," *Shambhala Sun*, September 2013, 54.

Lost Words

35 **"I put it away so carefully . . ."**: *Irish Times*, September 2, 2013, 1.

The Labyrinth of Exertion

40 **From the angle**: Francis Dojun Cook, *How to Raise an Ox: Zen Practice as Taught in Master Dogen's Shobogenzo* (Wisdom, 2002), Kindle edition, 43.

We immerse ourselves totally: Cook, extract from *How to Raise and Ox*, Wisdom Books website, http://www.wisdombooks.com/ProductExtract.asp?PID=14807.

Being Right

43 **"When you come rising in me . . ."**: Jane Hirshfield, "To Opinion," *After* (HarperCollins, 2006), 41.

44 **Our happiness and the happiness**: Thich Nhat Hanh, *The Heart of the Buddha's Teaching* (Parallax, 1998), 51.

Ordinary Things

47 Jane Hirshfield, "A Cedary Fragrance," *Poetry Foundation* website, http://www.poetryfoundation.org/features/audioitem/470.

No Thank-You

52 **In his book**: John Daido Loori, *Bringing the Sacred to Life: The Daily Practice of Zen Ritual* (Shambhala, 2008), 7.

A Space for Contemplation

59 **"There is great beauty and peace . . ."**: Thomas Merton, *The Intimate Merton: His Life from His Journals*, ed. Patrick Hart and Jonathan Montaldo (HarperSanFrancisco, 1995), 239, 284.

The Steady Go of the World

61 **More simply, the Zen teacher**: Shohaku Okumura, *Living By Vow: A Practical Introduction to Eight Essential Zen Chants and Texts* (Wisdom, 2012), Kindle edition, locations 3910, 1293, 1598, 3861.

62 **"We think our own life . . ."**: Okumura, *Realizing Genjokoan* (Wisdom, 2010), Kindle edition, location 1261.

And, as the poet Seamus Heaney demonstrates: Seamus Heaney, *Electric Light* (Farrar, Straus & Giroux, 2001), 4.

Well-met in Belfast

70 **And in his book**: Norman Fischer, *Taking Our Places: The Buddhist Path to Truly Growing Up* (HarperSanFrancisco, 2003), 9-10, 3.

71 **Mary Rose O'Reilly**: Mary Rose O'Reilley, *Radical Presence: Teaching as Contemplative Practice* (Boynton/Cook, 1998), 19, 21.

"We cannot only be passive listeners . . .": Fischer, 48, 51.

Lessons of the Selfie

74 **We mistake what Joseph Goldstein**: Joseph Goldstein, *Mindfulness: A Practical Guide to Awakening* (Sounds True, 2013), Kindle edition, 36.

"A cloud can never die . . .": Thich Nhat Hahn, *Beyond the Self: Teachings on the Middle Way* (Parallax, 2010), xiii.

Call it a Notion

76 **"Looking deeply into the wrong perceptions . . ."**: Thich Nhat Hanh, *Beyond the Self: Teachings on the Middle Way* (Parallax, 2010), 8, 12.

77 **In Ireland**: Stan Carey, "Not a Notion about Irish Notions," *Sentence First: An Irishman's Blog about the English Language* (https://stancarey.wordpress.com/2014/02/12/not-a-notion-about-irish-notions/).

As Joseph Goldstein reminds us: Joseph Goldstein, *Mindfulness* (Sounds True, 2013), Kindle edition, 268.

Making Whole

81 **Can we remember that pain**: Roshi Pat Enkyo O'Hara, *Most Intimate: A Zen Approach to Life's Challenges* (Shambhala, 2014), Kindle edition, 79.

Anything Can Happen Anytime

82 **Since then, he has found it**: Joseph Goldstein, *Mindfulness* (Sounds True, 2013), Kindle edition, 280.

Let's Not Go There

85 **"People ask us . . ."**: James Silas Rogers, *Northern Orchards: Notes from Places Near the Dead* (North Star Press of St. Cloud, 2014), 57.

86 **In his book:** Norman Fischer, *Training in Compassion: Zen Teachings on the Practice of Lojong* (Shambhala, 2012), 134.

Yeah, Whatever

89 **Those who looked at the world**: *Neurology*, May 28, 2014.

Put It in Neutral

94 **In zazen, the restless activity**: Jan Chozen Bays, "The Paradox of Prayer," *Buddhadharma*, Fall 2014, 39.

Not Two, Not One

97 **Concepts such as high and low**: Thich Nhat Hanh, *The Sun My Heart* (Parallax, 1988), 45.

98 **Each of us reflects**: Stephanie Kaza, *Mindfully Green: A Personal and Spiritual Guide to Whole Earth Thinking* (Shambhala, 2008), 44.

Immovable Awareness

100 **Katsuki Sekida**: Katsuki Sekida, *Two Zen Classics* (Weatherhill, 1977), 97.

101 **Have you ever noticed**: Jon Kabat-Zinn, *Coming to Our Senses* (Hyperion, 2006), 88, 90.

O Great Mystery

104 **How, asks Larry Abbott**: James Gorman, "Learning How Little We Know About the Brain," *New York Times*, November 10, 2014.

105 **What Zen does offer**: Shunryu Suzuki, *Zen Mind, Beginner's Mind* (Weatherhill, 1970), 116.

The Book of Janet

109 **As the Zen priest Norman Fischer**: Zoketsu Norman Fischer, "Love + Wisdom = Buddha," *Shambhala Sun*, January 2015, 58.

The Silence Around the Words

111 **But as Father Richard Rohr**: Father Richard Rohr, "Finding God in the Depths of Silence," Festival of Faiths, May, 2013. https://www.youtube.com/watch?v=uaMVKnpsDA8.

112 "Maisie at Dawn" is used by permission of Wake Forest University Press and the Random House Group (Jonathan Cape). The poem appears in Michael Longley's collection *The Stairwell* (Wake Forest University Press, 2014). *The Stairwell* was originally published in the UK by Jonathan Cape. Cf. Michael Longley's poem "Private Ungaretti" in the same volume: "We / Hear the din of battle / In the white silence / Around his words."

Healing is Possible

114 The Parable of the Burning House appears in the third chapter of *The Lotus Sutra*. See *The Lotus Sutra*, tr. Burton Watson (Columbia University Press, 1993), 62-69.

I was reminded of this parable: Allan Lokos, *Through the Flames: Overcoming Disaster through Compassion, Patience, and Determination* (Penguin, 2015).

116 **A pilot brought a plane down**: Lokos, Kindle Edition, 132.

Ethical Attentiveness

119 **To be human is to inhabit**: Sangharakshita, *Living with Awareness: A Guide to the Satipatthana Sutra* (Windhorse, 2012), 14-15.

120 **"One thing you need to remember..."**: Sayadaw U Tejaniya's comment is quoted by Joseph Goldstein in *Mindfulness* (Sounds True, 2013), Kindle edition, 103.

Living with Dignity

122 **For Buddhism the innate dignity**: Bhikkhu Bodhi, "Giving Dignity to Life," *Access to Insight* (Legacy Edition), 5 June 2010.

No matter how we want to cling: Sakyong Mipham, *Turning the Mind into an Ally* (Riverhead, 2003), 150.

True Intimacy

129 **"Intimacy,"** writes the Zen teacher Jakusho Kwong: Jakusho Kwong, *No Beginning, No End: The Intimate Heart of Zen* (Harmony, 2003), 111.

131 **When we open our awareness**: Shohaku Okumura, *Living by Vow* (Shambhala, 2010), 70.

The Music of Constancy

133 **"As everyone knows . . ."**: Herman Melville, *Moby-Dick*, (Random House, 1950), 2.

Ishmael is not a meditative practitioner: Daniel Herman, *Zen and the White Whale* (Lehigh University Press, 2014), 35.

134 **In its presence, we can readily observe**: Seamus Heaney, "Perch," *Electric Light* (Farrar, Straus and Giroux, 2001), 4.

135 **"Written on water," one might say**: Charles Tomlinson, *Written on Water* (Oxford 1972), 54.

Soft Eyes

139 **In *The Breathing Book***: Donna Farhi, *The Breathing Book* (Henry Holt, 1996), 103-104.

And in *Centered Riding*: Sally Swift, *Centered Riding* (St. Martin's, 1985), 11.

The Study of Silence

141 **In her book *Reclaiming Conversation***: Sherry Turkle, *Reclaiming Conversation: The Power of Talk in a Digital Age* (Penguin, 2015), 38f.

NOTES

And as Thich Nhat Hanh observes: Thich Nhat Hanh, *Silence: The Power of Quiet in a World Full of Noise* (HarperOne, 2015), 22–24.

142 **Father Richard Rohr**: Father Richard Rohr, "Finding God in the Depths of Silence," Festival of Faiths, May, 2013. https://www.youtube.com/watch?v=uaMVKnpsDA8.

The physicist George Prochnik: George Prochnik, *In Pursuit of Silence* (Anchor, 2010), Kindle edition, 235, 289.

143 **We also open ourselves**: Shizuteru Ueda, "Silence and Words in Zen Buddhism," *Diogenes*, no. 170, vol. 43/2, Summer, 1995.

A Mind that Alights Nowhere

145 **As a boy growing up**: "Surely goodness and mercy shall follow me all the days of my life, and I will dwell in the house of the Lord forever" (*Psalm* 23:6).

147 **And over time, Zen teachings promise**: "All Bodhisattvas should develop a pure, lucid mind that doesn't depend on sight, sound, touch, flavor, smell or any thought that arises in it. A Bodhisattva should develop a mind that alights nowhere. The mind should be kept independent of any thoughts that arise within it. If the mind depends upon anything, it has no sure haven" (*The Diamond Sutra*, 14).

Give It All Away

149 **What is Zen? Stop now**: Shinge Roko Sherry Chayat Roshi, "What is Zen?" Zen Center of Syracuse website. http://www.zencenterofsyracuse.org/content/what-is-zen.

151 **"Wherever you are," wrote Shunryu Suzuki Roshi**: Shunryu Suzuki Roshi, quoted by Zenkei Blanche Hartman, *Seeds for a Boundless Life* (Shambhala, 2015), 34.

We are also, in the phrase of Zoketsu Norman Fischer: Norman Fischer, *Training in Compassion* (Shambhala, 2012).

The Gift of Non-Fear

153 **The gift of non-fear**: "There are three kinds of gifts—the gift of material resources, the gift of helping people rely on themselves, and the gift of non-fear. Helping people not be destroyed by fear is the greatest gift of all." Thich Nhat Hanh, *Touching Peace* (Parallax, 1992), 83-84.

Can we "turn toward [our] fears": Zenkei Blanche Hartman, *Seeds for a Boundless Life* (Shambhala, 2015), 69

But if we are in need: Michele McDonald: *RAIN - DROP: Recognition, Acceptance, Investigation, and Non-Identification and their opposites: Delusion, Resistance, Indifference, and Personification*. Michele McDonald's Dharma Talks. http://dharmaseed.org/teacher/126/

See also Jack Kornfield's discussion of R.A.I.N. in *The Wise Heart: A Guide to the Universal Teachings of Buddhist Psychology* (Bantam, 2008), 101-107, and Tara Brach's detailed instructions in *True Refuge: Finding Peace and Freedom in Your Own Awakened Heart* (Bantam, 2013), 61-76.

A Permanent Beginning

158 **The first moment of wonder**: *The Essential Brendan Kennelly*, ed. Terence Brown and Michael Longley (Wake Forest, 2011), includes a CD of poems read by Brendan Kennelly. Kennelly's remarks on poetry have been transcribed from that recording.

What It Means to be Present

161 **In his book The Four-Dimensional Human**: Laurence Scott, *The Four-Dimensional Human: Ways of Being in the Digital World* (Heinemann, 2015), 26, 24, 14; 4. My italics.

"Presence is not some exotic state": Tara Brach, *True Refuge: Finding Peace and Freedom in Your Own Awakened Heart* (Bantam, 2013), 12.

A Time to Let Go

174 **"How much are you playing"**: Stuart Jeffries, "I'm a better musician now than when I was 70," *The Guardian*, Friday, September 13, 2013.

One Particular Action

172 **Partly because**: Louis MacNeice, "Autumn Journal," *The Collected Poems of Louis MacNeice* (Faber, 1966), 132-133.

173 **The simplest formulation**: Norman Fischer and Susan Moon, *What is Zen?* (Shambhala, 2016), 61-63.

174 **According to the oft-cited findings**: Benjamin Libet, "Unconscious cerebral initiative and the role of conscious will in voluntary action," *Behavioral and Brain Sciences*, vol. 8, 1985, 529-566.

Participants in the Belfast retreat: Norman Fischer, *Taking Our Places* (HarperSanFrancisco, 2003), 58-59.

My Unexpected Teacher

176 An earlier version of this essay first appeared in *Buddhadharma* (Summer 2008).

* * *

All of the essays in this collection first appeared in the *Alfred Sun*, the community newspaper of Alfred, New York. My thanks to David Snyder, editor, for his continuing support.

About the Author

Poet and essayist Ben Howard was born in 1944 and grew up in eastern Iowa. His interest in Buddhist meditation originated in the 1970s, kindled by the prose of Peter Matthiessen and the poems of Gary Snyder. Having learned the fundamentals of sitting practice from Allen Ginsberg in 1978, he became a student of Vipassana meditation and later of Vietnamese Rinzai Zen, as taught by the Venerable Thich Nhat Hanh. More recently, he has studied Japanese Rinzai Zen with Jiro Osho Fernando Afable and Shinge Roko Sherry Chayat Roshi. In 2002 he received the *jukai* precepts in the Hakuin/Torei lineage of Rinzai Zen at Dai Bosatsu Zendo. Since 1998 he has led the Falling Leaf Sangha, a Zen practice group in Alfred, New York.

Howard holds a doctorate in English Literature from Syracuse University, where he studied with Donald Justice, Philip Booth, and William Wasserstrom. Before his retirement in 2006, he taught literature, writing, classical guitar, and Buddhist meditation at Alfred University. Over the past four decades he has contributed poems, essays, articles, and reviews to literary journals here and abroad, including *Poetry*, the *Sewanee Review*, *Poetry Ireland Review*, and *Shenandoah*. The author of ten previous books, he has been the recipient of numerous awards, including the Milton Dorfman Prize in Poetry and a fellowship from the National Endowment for the Arts. He lives with his wife, Robin Caster Howard, in the village of Alfred.

www.ingramcontent.com/pod-product-compliance
Lightning Source LLC
Chambersburg PA
CBHW022105040426
42451CB00007B/129